In Keeping With The Wolves

IN KEEPING WITH THE WOLVES

Charlie Bamforth

pemandos

First published in Great Britain in 1992 by
Pemandos A & M, The Haven, Little Hay, Lichfield,
Staffordshire, on behalf of Charles Bamforth.

ISBN 0 95 20314 0 X

FOREWORD

Reading this book by Charlie Bamforth, "In Keeping with the Wolves", reminded me of the occasion I kept goal myself on the Molineux. I had been staying with my old friend Roy Pritchard and "digging" with his landlady in Whitmore Reams. That week I had played, wearing the number 6 shirt, in a practise match and was told by the manager at that time, Ted Vizard, to report on the Saturday for a full blown practise match.

This was in early August 1946. The dressing room was quite full of established players and some time elapsed before I knew what was happening. Eventually Ted Vizard approached and said, "can you keep goal". Out I went and the game ended 1-1 and I think my ambition to be a professional footballer seemed to evaporate there and then.

I returned to the first eleven at Loughborough College, who then played in the Leicestershire Senior League, but whenever possible I went to Molineux to watch the fortunes of Wolves, and indeed saw many of the goalkeepers who are included in these pages.

I hope that you will also relive a memory when you read this book as I have while enjoying the stories these Wolves goalkeepers have told through Charlie.

Jack Harris.

This book is dedicated to the father I never knew, but in whose memory I became devoted to Wolverhampton Wanderers Football Club.

CONTEXT

I had plenty of time to see the ball. It didn't so much hurtle through the sodden air as gently waft. Down I went, splat! into the quagmire of my six-yard-box, like some hippopotamus overdue a good stint at a health farm. Thwack! went the ball as it smacked against my greasy palms and squelched agonisingly back from whence it had arrived. Thanks! grinned the astonished centre-forward as he gleefully stabbed the rebound well away from my grovelling, simpering form and into the gaping net.

As I staggered to my feet, the first person I espied through mud-splattered spectacles secured to my balding head by a straining piece of elastic was our centre-half. Here, too, was a veritable superstar of the Sunday football world, a man for whom training comprised a subtle blend of darts and draught Bass. With cultivated Geordie intonation he proclaimed:

"Wai, plonka! 'av sin sum crap gowalkeypin in ma tyme, but tha' teks the biskit!"

"Come on, grandad!" yelled our fan as I shaped to hoof the next clearance away. The ball left a leaden boot, barely to reach the halfway line.

There was nothing for it: I knew then and there that my goalkeeping career had come to an ignominious conclusion. I was 31.

As numbed and frozen fingers struggled to slacken caked laces from clagged boots, I inconsolably thought back to the endless hours as a child when I would hurl a burst and mis-shapen ball against a wall, diving to catch it without a thought about the concrete terrain.

Did I not come from the outskirts of Wigan from whence a succession of fine keepers like Wilf Birkett, Fred Else, John Barton and David Gaskell had leaped forth, all to find different shades of glory at a fledgling age?

Night after night my head would hit the pillow with thoughts of emulating my Wolverhampton heroes: Malcolm Finlayson, Fred Davies and later, above all, Phil Parkes. Despite being eighty miles away, Wolves were my team - through them I could reach the father who had died before I was born. They had been his team, I was told.

Time went by. A rugby-playing school got in the way, but above all else an obsession with perambulating about the countryside watching my heroes when I'd have been better-advised playing myself, meant that the dream remained just that.

And so, as I kicked off my boots for the last time, I had precious little to look back on by way of my own performances. Instead there were a host of memories about the various players that had the great good fortune to achieve what was my own personal Utopia: to keep goal for Wolverhampton Wanderers.

They do say that those that can, do. Those that can't teach - or preach - or write. It's the next best thing.

For me, then, it was an acceptable fall-back to have the great good fortune to write a column for the Wolverhampton Wanderers programme from 1985 to 1990. I loved every minute of it.

Not so much, however, as bringing the writing and the goalkeeping together in this small book. To meet a host of idols in the course of compiling this volume has been, quite simply, a joy. They have all been most helpful, most kind. All of them gave of their time quite freely to talk to me, each aware that any proceeds accruing to me are being devoted to charity. It was too much a labour of love for it to be otherwise.

Some goalkeepers I couldn't reach or trace and that is to my regret. Others, who shall remain nameless, repeatedly failed to respond to my pleas for help.

But help, most certainly, was forthcoming from many folk. Sincere thanks to Jack Harris for kindly writing the Forward to this book - another Wolves goalkeeper! I acknowledge the assistance of Peter Creed from the Express and Star who guided me to many former players. As ever, Dot Wooldridge from behind the scenes at Molineux was superbly helpful to me. Bill and Denise Plum provided many excellent photographs, as, too, did the Express & Star. Thanks, too, to Fred Kemp, J.C. McGinn (chairman of Celtic), and Margaret at the Tranmere training centre for their assistance in reaching players. Don Stanton and his staff at Pemandos were, as normal, superb. My good friend Mike Nicholson checked any potential libels!!

Perhaps above all, though, I must mention my long-suffering wife, Diane, and my children Peter and Caroline. Squeezing in a book at the end of long days at work is daunting for writer and family alike, taking as it does one away to a lonely tip-tapping word processor. Diane snapped just the once - but the teapot didn't break and I wasn't scalded! She's a veritable football widow and I can only say how much I appreciate her tolerance.

I hope you enjoy the book. It's a pity you didn't see me as a goalkeeper!

Charlie Bamforth

Wisborough Green, October, 1992.

CONTENTS

IL GATTONE

The Italian team couldn't believe their eyes. They'd come to White Hart Lane oozing confidence and it was no surprise when they relentlessly bore down on the England goal. Seventy thousand spectators, the majority desperate for a home victory, held their breath in the chill November air as the blue shirts threatened an avalanche of goals.

The mighty Italians, however, reigning World Champions, had not reckoned on the heroic gymnastics of a modest blond goalkeeper, who broke their hearts - and their spirit. That man was Bert Williams, earning his fourth cap and about to be christened by the admiring Italians 'Il Gattone' - The Big Cat.

Time and again the Midlander, who revelled in the spectacular, appeared to defy gravity as he sprang with feline grace to deflect, to catch, to repel allcomers. Inspired by their custodian, the England team took full advantage and Wolverhampton-born Jack Rowley, together with Billy Wright, Williams' skipper for club and country, struck the goals which brought the host nation a memorable victory.

To this day you will hear the older of the fanatical Italian footballing fraternity speak in awe about the fearless keeper that shut them out in 1949. They may not quite so readily recite the full England team:

Williams (Wolves); Alf Ramsey (Spurs); Johnny Aston (Manchester United); Willie Watson (Sunderland); Neil Franklin (Stoke City); Wright (Wolves); Tom Finney (Preston North End); Stan Mortensen (Blackpool); Rowley (Manchester United); Stan Pearson (Manchester United); Jack Froggatt (Portsmouth).

Bert Williams smiles unassumingly when you recall his nickname.

"Yes, that's what they called me - amongst other things!"

But he could handle whatever they hurled at him, for he genuinely loved the game. He always had, since the days as a nipper when he played for St Martin's school in his home village of Bradley, near Bilston.

"I knew then that I wanted to play the game. Money didn't come into it. I was always a goalkeeper - I couldn't head a ball to save my life!"

Bert, who was born on 31st January 1920, also played for Bilston Boys and recalls that

"I wasn't too bad academically, but everything I thought about was sport. I was pretty good at Composition - what you'd call English Language today - so I thought that perhaps I could make a sports reporter. But playing the game is what I really loved and, in that, I was greatly encouraged by my father."

Walter Williams had himself been a good class goalkeeper, playing for Coseley Athletic. But the need to play in spectacles inhibited his career. Walter Williams was determined that young Bert would have a better chance.

"Due to him I first got a game at Walsall. It was a twist of fate - a lot of players far better than I didn't get such an opportunity. I've been very fortunate. My father was friendly with a local publican whose son, in turn, was a friend of Andy Wilson, then manager at Fellows Park. That was how Walsall got to hear of me and, sure enough, one Friday evening they came to Bradley desperately short of a keeper for the reserve team in next day's Birmingham Combination game. I was 15.

"I'd left school a year earlier and was working for the engineering company Thompson Brothers at Great Bridge. They had an exceptional side in the Wolverhampton Works League, with four or five semi-professionals. Luckily I got into the team, even though I was very much on the small side, which was a really sore point with me."

Bert Williams leans forward, resting folded arms on his dining room table, his eyes reflecting the worry of those days and the agony of the repeated stretching exercises which Peter Shilton in later years became so well known for. The exercises undoubtedly worked and, to Bert Williams' relief, they expanded his frame to a highly suitable 5 foot 10½ inches.

"Every week I would pore through a book called Topical Times and would be delighted if someone had asked a question on the letters page about how tall Harry Hibbs was."

The great Birmingham City goalkeeper was a well-known little 'un - if he could make the grade to such good effect then perhaps there was hope for young Bert.

"And there was Jim Barron at Blackburn (father of the future Wolves keeper) who, like Hibbs, stood about 5 foot 8 inches. It's to their credit that they became such fine goalkeepers. In those days sides tended to be selected with the biggest and hardest in goal as there was a lot of knocking about. There's no comparison today - the rules are different! When Nat Lofthouse and Trevor Ford were around you knew you'd be hit in mid-air. You expected that if you came down with two feet you'd be shoulder-charged. It's good to a certain extent that goalkeepers are better protected these days, but it's gone to an extreme. And just total up how much time a keeper wastes nowadays. We'd have to get rid of the ball quickly or else it was in the back of the net and you with it! Today there's no reason why a goalkeeper shouldn't play on until he's 45. Only injury should get in his way and there's less chance of that because they don't go down at opponents' feet anywhere near as often as we used to."

So it was a tough trade that the 14-year-old Williams yearned for as he hung from the bannisters of his home. For inspiration he'd study the keepers of his favourite club West Bromwich Albion and those that came with the visiting sides.

"I well remember watching Elisha Scott and Harry Hibbs playing at The Hawthorns. West Brom had Harold Pearson in goal, whose father Hubert was goalie before him. There was Trentham at left back, who always played with a hankie in his hand. As kids we'd copy him!"

To this day Bert Williams can recite perfectly the Baggies' Cup Final side of 1935.

"At Thompson's there was an Albion scout, with whom I pleaded for a trial. He was insistent that I was too small. He laughed about it years later when I met up with him as a Wolves player."

Wolverhampton Wanderers, though, were still a dream when the young Williams signed amateur forms for Walsall. At seventeen he turned professional for £1 per week and was soon called into the senior side for his Third Division (South) debut with Bristol City.

"Walsall had two senior keepers at the time in McSevich and Ken Tewkesbury, the Amateur international. The trainer Harry Waite's son was a goalkeeper too. Harry was a nice fellow, really helpful. Andy Wilson, too, the old Scottish international, spent hours shooting at me. It was Andy that gave me my first chance."

War intervened with Bert Williams' career, though, just as it did with that of so many other promising young professional footballers. It can be argued, however, that it was the making of him.

"When War came I thought 'it can't be for long'. I volunteered for the RAF and became a PTI, which suited me admirably. Before long I was a corporal and then a sargeant. There were lots of pro footballers as PTI's and I learned such a lot from the likes of Frank O'Donnell and Jack Acquaroff. I was stationed all over the place -Uxbridge, Cosford, Ludford Magna, Tangmere, Lichfield, Wing. Whilst I was at Wing I guested for Chelsea, who badly wanted me to sign for them. I also guested for Nottingham Forest and Lincoln City but would hitch-hike home at every opportunity: I've always been a home bird.

"At the end of the War I came back to Walsall and was told one day that in the Board Room there was a representative of a big club who wanted to sign me. I automatically assumed that it would be someone from Chelsea; in fact it was Jack Howley, the famous secretary from the Wolves. 'I'm awfully sorry', I told him, 'I'd like to sign for Chelsea'. Jack spoke to me for an hour and was so nice and helpful. He implored me to go home and talk to my wife about the situation, which I agreed to do.

"When I got home I discovered that, whilst combing her hair, my wife had somehow cut her eye. That was when it struck me that it wouldn't be the best thing in the world if that sort of thing had happened if I was in London whilst she was up in the Midlands. So I signed for Wolves!"

The fee was reputed to be £3,500.

Bert Williams acknowledges the part which fate has to play in anyone's career. ("I probably wouldn't have been successful at Stamford Bridge - they didn't win much".) Fate certainly dealt a good card into the Williams hand that day in September, 1945 when he signed on the dotted line for Wolves, for he was destined to play a masterful role in the glorious Wanderers side of the late forties and early fifties.

"Ironically, my first game for Wolves was against Chelsea in the Football League (South) in 1945-1946. I've still got the cutting, which shows that I had a fair game. It's my wife that started the scrapbooks - only recently did I finish putting all the bits and pieces in. People say to me: what about all your old jerseys, caps and so on? Frankly, the only time I see them is when I move house! I had put a load into a box in the shed and the mice made a nice nest in them! There's nothing about the house to show anything about my career.

"If you recall, Bill Shorthouse and Roy Swinbourne retired at the same time as me in 1957 and we were each honoured to receive a silver tray from the people of Wolverhampton. I'd put mine away somewhere -until Roy told me he'd had his valued at £6,000!"

Small wonder that the people of the town chose to honour their immensely popular keeper in this way. For hadn't he been their custodian in the victorious cup winning side of 1949, when Leicester had been summarily dispatched 3-1? Wasn't he still there when Wanderers lifted their first Championship trophy in 1954? And when could they ever forget the thrilling floodlit friendly matches when the cream of international club soccer came to Molineux to be put in their place by a Wolves team featuring arguably the best goalkeeper in England?

I insert the word 'arguably' only because Bert Williams will want it that way, for his modesty is immense.

"There were so many good goalkeepers around at the time - I admired Bert Trautmann, Sam Bartram, Ted Ditchburn, Jack Fairbrother. But there was no doubt that the best I ever saw was Frank Swift. Strong in the air and on the ground, a good kicker - but most of all he was the life and soul of the party, a real comedian. When we were on England tours he'd sit Stan Mortensen on his knee with his hand up the back of his jacket and they'd do a ventriloquist act! When we were on a transport plane with a trap door in the middle, he'd have everyone walking gingerly around that door, convinced that if they trod on it they'd shoot out!"

Williams' big rival for the England job was Gilbert Merrick, the moustachioed successor to Hibbs at St Andrews, as Bert points out when he recalls his early international career.

Bert's first appearance for England as a Wolves player (he had previously appeared whilst on Walsall's books) was in a Wartime international, drawn 2-2 with France in May 1945. Five months later he had good cause to remember the 1-0 defeat which his England team suffered at The Hawthorns, for Wales' keeper that day was a colleague at Molineux, Cyril Sidlow.

When peacetime football resumed, Frank Swift was esconced in the yellow goalkeeper's jersey of England and Bert Williams had to wait until May 1949 for his first full cap in a 3-1 defeat of France in Paris. Except for one match where Luton's Bernard Streten stood between the posts, Williams kept his place for two and a half years, before Merrick stepped into the fray. The Big Cat would stalk the England area again - but not for over three years, in which time England had suffered the ignominy of those historic 6-3 and 7-1 drubbings at the hands of the mighty Hungarians. Bert was on the bench as a substitute for the former game at Wembley.

"To be honest, it broke my heart to see it. England were humiliated."

But Bert will not criticise Merrick's role in that defeat.

"He and I had different styles. I used to revel in getting to the 'impossible'. To me the secret of good goalkeeping is to get some part of your body behind the ball at all times. Basically abiding by this principle made me look acrobatic. Gilbert's style, I suppose, was less spectacular. Anything that was within dropping distance on either side of him was his."

Perhaps, then, it is no surprise that one of Bert Williams' most treasured memories is the night that Wolves beat Honved, featuring eight of the Hungarian national side, by 3-2 just seven months after England's 7-1 humbling in Budapest.

"We all did very well. It was being broadcast on radio and the match went on a few seconds after nine o'clock. The BBC decided that the game shouldn't interfere with the news, so with a Honved forward running through with only me to beat they announced 'Here is the 9 o'clock news'! Apparently the lines were red hot from people wanting to know what had happened at Molineux."

Bert Williams, of course, dived at the forward's feet and the ball bounced away for Bill Slater to clear. Thus the game was sensationally won, a game which at half time had been going in the Hungarians' favour by two clear goals. A full house at Molineux that night saw the following Wolves team christened by newspapers the unofficial 'Champions of the World':

Bert Williams; Eddie Stuart; Bill Shorthouse; Bill Slater; Billy Wright; Ron Flowers; Johnny Hancocks(1); Peter Broadbent; Roy Swinbourne(2); Dennis Wilshaw; Leslie Smith.

Another game which stands out for Bert is the 1949 F.A.Cup semi-final with Manchester United at Hillsborough.

"Both of our fullbacks, Laurie Kelly and Roy Pritchard, were injured and could hardly walk. Somehow we managed to draw and, in the replay, we had two backs in Alf Crook and Terry Springthorpe who had hardly played before. We won 1-0 at Goodison in an excellent game, but tragically Alf was injured at Liverpool four days later and never played again.

"To be honest, though, what stand out in my memory are the things that went wrong! There was that game in Belo Horizonte when England lost to the U.S.A. 1-0 when we should have won about ten. There was the game against Bournemouth when we lost 1-0 and the goalposts collapsed. I remember Stan Matthews beating me in one match - that was annoying because he didn't get many! I took it as an insult if I let a goal in - I've been upset millions of times! It was a personal affront - it used to worry me terribly. Being so consciencious probably made me into a better keeper: you must have pride and standards.

"Then there was the occasion at Goodison in Ted Vizard's day when, with two minutes to go, I came running out to belt the ball away at the edge of the box. I remember thinking 'it'll take 'em a couple of minutes to get this one back'. I sliced it for a corner from which Everton scored. Nobody blamed me afterwards - but I felt so upset.

"Those feelings soon passed, for I was extremely happy at Wolves. It was the club for me. You had to be on your toes, though - we had possibly seventy or more professionals on the books at any one time. Dennis Parsons and Ted Elliott were there in reserve. Then there was Nigel Sims who was an extremely good goalkeeper and also 'Paddy' Dwyer."

Bert Williams, however, thrived on the challenge. His fitness was a key feature of his game - he spent hour after hour doing physical training and running. As a sprinter he had few peers. Whilst in the RAF he came second at the White City to McDonald Bailey, the world champion. Arthur Wint, too, narrowly defeated him in another race. After taking part in a match at Cosford, it was suggested to him that he participate in the subsequent championships at Molineux. Despite Bert's protestations that he couldn't, being a professional footballer, he was entered. Sure enough, the disqualification came and Bert never ran again, despite being asked to run the legendary Powderhall sprint.

"I spent hours on physical fitness - it was an obsession. But you never get something for nothing. I never went to a dance as a player - sacrifices had to be made."

At the end of the 1956-1957 season, Bert Williams decided to call it a day.

"It was a matter of principle really. During the year we used to go away for special training. By now, I had started my sports business and having to go away for a couple of weeks at a time obviously took me away from it for excessive periods. A choice had to be made. I was 37 years old remember.

"Wolves didn't want me to retire and, in retrospect, it was one of the worst decisions of my life. You miss playing so much. I could possibly have played for another three or four years, being so fit. But I didn't want to be left destitute with no prospects, so I put my business first. Three or four clubs wanted me to sign for them, but the answer was always no. I wanted to finish at the top. I never kicked a ball again. In fact I didn't go to see many games: it was such a wrench to watch it: I wanted to be playing, too!"

Bert Williams had always thrown himself into the fray fully as a goalkeeper. Now it was time to dive headlong into his new life as a sports shop owner and head of his own sports centre ahead of its time at Bilston. It had all the equipment, including three indoor cricket wickets, squash court, boxing ring as well as the shop and warehouse which supplied schools up and down the land. But the Bert Williams School was noted especially as the first goalkeeping centre of excellence.

"We could take twenty - the first to apply, though we had three or four hundred letters. One lad hitched from the States and arrived the day we packed up for the Summer! Joe Corrigan, Phil Parkes (the West Ham one), Geoff Crudgington, Fred Davies - I helped them all. On top of that I'd go to Manchester City to help Joe; to Birmingham with Jim Herriot and to Coventry to work, amongst others, with David Icke! Night after night I'd hit shots at the youngsters until eventually I cut the inside of my bladder doing just that. We'd take kids off the street and coach them for free. Then one Sunday the place caught fire. It was time to sell up."

Bert did just that - to the former Baggies keepers Jim Cumbes and John Osborne - and bought land at Shifnal, where he built factories rented out to engineering concerns.

To this day Bert is in business, with his two sons. He also has a daughter. All live local to Bert, near Shifnal. Both of his grandchildren, James and Clare, are at university. He freely admits that "life has been very good to me."

That prosaic chronicler of Wolves' history, Percy Young, once wrote of Williams:

Such grace, poise, agility and daring had not, perhaps, heretofore been seen; not, that is, so combined with modesty and integrity both on and off the field.

Young's description is perfect. For to this day the quick eyes and classic profile of the immaculate blond Williams are complimented by a gentleness and correctness of speech which refuse to speak ill of anyone. He picks his words cautiously when asked to describe latter day goalkeepers.

"On occasions Grobbelaar looks good - and then he makes such a hash of a cross. Basically Shilton is still one of the best - he is very correct. He must train hard - a man after my own heart. Neville Southall probably has the edge on him now, though. But I just don't like seeing them with those big gloves on these days. Maier used to make me cringe! At the goalkeeping school I used to turn my back on them and I could hear if they were catching the ball properly. If it slaps against the hands, it'll be dropped. There's only one way to catch a ball..."

and Williams demonstrates.

"I used to love to come to the edge of my 18-yard-line to catch the ball. Taking those high ones gave you so much confidence. These days it should be even easier to do it.

"The secret of good goalkeeping is to keep your head high and be quick on your feet. Even if the ball was going past me I'd keep my eye on it - until it hit the net!"

* * * * * * * * * *

When Wolves played Moscow Dynamo in August 1989 in the re-run of the historic floodlit friendly between the two sides 34 years earlier, Bert Williams was one of many famous ex-Wanderers invited to the game. He was intrigued to meet a man called David Hough, lifelong Wolves supporter, who is surely Bert's greatest fan. David lives in Manchester, where to this day he maintains his stance that one goalkeeper surpassed all others. "If your book has 100 pages, then 99 of them should be devoted to Bert Williams. People get sick of me telling them what a marvellous player he was. But quite simply he was the greatest. He still is."

"THERE'S NOBODY ELSE"

"People have said to me: 'you're an arrogant bugger'. But, you see, a goalkeeper has to be. You're on your own out there. And the other lads in the team - it was a case of 'how's the big man today?' 'Great', I would say, 'I'm really feeling good about this one today'. And that would make them feel good, too. It was what they wanted to hear. That sort of talk from a keeper bouys them. They don't want a keeper whose knees are knocking the whole time."

Nigel Sims drew again on his cigarette and smiled. I'd asked him whether he rated many of the modern day goalkeepers.

"I don't think so" he replied, sardonically. I haven't seen much of Woods, but let's face it, if there'd been much around then Shilton wouldn't still have been in the England goal. Shilton! A trained goalkeeper. No - give me a natural. They can work hard too, you know. Shilton's like a robot. And to think that Matt Gillies let Banksy go from Leicester and put Shilton in. There's no comparison!"

Nigel Sims himself was a natural. He was, quite simply, a great keeper, whose sole recognition was two call-ups to the Football League representative XI.

"If you ask me for my honest opinion, then I'll tell you that I was the best about for eight years. But I had no chance, had I? Arthur Oakley, Wolves' chairman, was chairman of the England selectors. No player who left Wolves got a look in."

Sims had left Wolves under sad circumstances. Under ten years earlier he had walked into Molineux on a dream.

'Nigger' was born in the village of Coton-in-the-Elms, in the shade of the breweries of Burton on Trent, on 9th August, 1931. As a lad he played for his village side in the local league, turning out in the forward line for the boy's team and in goal for the senior side. Father, who ran the club, enquired of Mr Duggan, who ran the local Edingale side and the Black Horse pub, and who was prominent in local soccer circles, what he thought of young Nigel: what was it to be, centre-forward or custodian? Duggan declared the latter. Shortly afterwards, the strapping young Sims was having a good 'un for Coton against Pirelli when he was spotted by Wolves scout Charlie Wheeler. A trial was arranged.

"The trainer Jack Smith had us kids playing against a local works side. They kicked us to bits - we lost 8-0! I thought 'well that's that' and told dad I'd had enough. Fortunately for me he advised patience and, of course, I was raring for another chance by the middle of the week. Next off we played Walsall's 'B' team -and lost 4-0!

"Years later I found out that, towards the end of the season, they were that desperate for keepers they looked down the list, my name cropped up and that's when they sent for me. It was 1947-1948. We played a game at Molineux against Stourbridge. Cullis had just taken over from Vizard. 'Would you like to join the groundstaff?' he asked me. What! How would you like a million pounds?! That's how I felt about it. I was only saying to The Finn (Malcolm Finlayson, Nigel Sims' great buddy) the other week - we'd have walked to Molineux, just to play for the Wolves.

"I'd been woodworking with Midland Timber in Burton. Now, as a 16-year-old, I was going to earn £4 a week at Wolves. My digs were £2 a week, with Mrs Llowarch in Vincent Street by the ground. She also had Jack Short, Ken Whitfield, Ian Clark and Johnny Walker, all good friends.

"Wolves had about eight teams in those days - I couldn't get a game in any of them. So I was off as twelfth man (no substitutes in those days) for the Reserves. We were playing at Blackpool. I was sitting at the front with the skip and heard such a commotion at the back. Ted Elliott, the goalkeeper, had gone down with food poisoning. 'I'm too ill - I can't play' I heard him groaning. And they'd reply 'you have to, Ted, there's nobody else'! But what about me! So that's how I got in - big Angus McLean, Roy Pritchard -they brought me through it. We drew, I think no goals. On the Monday I'd moved up to training with the reserves and first team. Things went well, so from then on I was reserve team keeper. Pure luck really."

Sims signed as a full-time professional in September 1948, for the handsome sum of £7 per week. Before the season was through he'd made it to the top.

"The Everall coach-owning brothers, Don and Cliff, were great Wolves fans. On Easter Monday, 1949 they picked me and also Dennis Parsons (another reserve keeper) up from home and took us to Bramall Lane. 'Bert's injured' we were told. I never thought much more about it, fully expecting Dennis to play. At 2.30 I was sat reading the programme when in walked Cullis. 'What are you doing?' he asked. 'Get your strip on!' he ordered. We drew 1-1."

Wolves' team, in front of 33,217 spectators, read:

Nigel Sims; Roy Pritchard; Terry Springthorpe; Bill Crook; Bill Shorthouse; Billy Wright; Johnny Hancocks; Sammy Smyth; Dennis Wilshaw; Jimmy Dunn; Jimmy Mullen (1).

"Bert Wiliams had hurt his hand and the speculation was that I might play in the F.A.Cup final. I played in the games up to the final, but Bert came back for Wembley.

"Bert wasn't really any help to me. Yes, we'd exercise together. But he would say that we were of different styles. Actually I reckon he had an eye on his place in the team!"

Sims' eyes twinkled impishly at this. He still has those sleepy eyes and ever-youthful good looks, bronzed by the sunshine at his home on the beautiful Gower in South Wales.

"But we were real goalkeepers, not like all those so-called worldbeaters in the World Cup. Did you see them? Beaten on the near post, beaten from daft freekicks. And the press and television were building them up so much. If we'd done the sort of things they do Cullis would have bloody hung, drawn and quartered us! If the ball is coming from the right it's obvious that the bloke's going to put it into the near post, unless he's a great and might glance it. But mostly it'll go to the near post - so that's what you cover. They don't these days! It's the percentage game. We spent hours and hours practising our angles. Cross after cross would be put over - there was no keeper at the Wolves who wasn't good at crosses - and those were the days when wingers really could put them over. We didn't have weaknesses - because if you did Cullis would make you practice till you lost those weaknesses! He bloody knew everything, Stan did!"

Another wry smile melted on Sims' lips in response to my question of how he got on with the legendary former Wolves supremo. After a momentary pause he replied.

"I always remember coming down through the town centre with my arm round a girl, purely innocently of course. Cullis came by - 'we'll have none of that' he stormed. We had to be in our digs by 10 o'clock at night. He didn't like people driving around in cars either! But I tell you this: I had seven years at Wolves and those years put me in good stead for the rest of my life. I learnt about attitude and discipline and to treat people as you would like to be treated. We worked bloody hard, too."

In 1949 Nigel went to do his National Service in the Royal Artillery at Rhyl and, later, Oswestry. Because he wasn't training with the senior players, Cullis made him play third team soccer and, as a consequence, he enjoyed just a solitary first team game for two seasons. Then it was a case of competition between Sims and Parsons for the green jersey when Williams was injured until Parsons moved on to the Villa in September 1952, leaving the young giant as undisputed second choice.

"But it got to the stage when I thought 'can I or can't I be a first division keeper?' Although Bert was a good friend - I played in his Bert Williams cricket XI - I honestly got irritated with the number of times he reckoned he was retiring. He was a highly strung type - and it was all very frustrating for me. So I went to see Cullis. 'I'm fed up with playing in the reserves' I told him. 'You think you're too good to play in my reserves, do you?' was his reply. 'Yes I do' I insisted. So he stuck me in the third team! I'd have been there now if Bert hadn't got injured."

By the time he left Molineux, Nigel Sims had played 38 Division One matches and once in the F.A. Cup, apart from scattered friendly games against the likes of Antwerp ("the first time I'd ever been abroad"), Brighton ("that time, in the Imperial in Brighton, I saw my first telly") and, more importantly, Glasgow Celtic and Maccabi of Tel Aviv in two of the prestigious Floodlit Friendlies of the fifties. He was also a substitute in the game against Spartak in Moscow in 1955.

"Fabulous. It was nothing like people had described it: the women were beautiful, honest!"

A year later, though, Sims and Cullis weren't talking. It was obvious that the parting of the ways was imminent. Sims duly signing for the Villa boss Eric Houghton, who paid £12,000 for the burly keeper's registration. Villa were deep in relegation territory, but Sims' arrival heralded a vast improvement in fortunes and the new keeper instantly became a great favourite with the crowd. The next manager wasn't to share that enthusiasm - but that was for the future, Sims having one of the finest games of his career in the 1957 Cup Final defeat of Busby's Babes.

"They reckoned we were no-hopers. But for the first twenty minutes we murdered them. Then Ray Wood got injured in that clash with McParland and it all went ragged. But Peter got those two goals and I can remember thinking 'bloody hell, I'm going to get a medal'. Then Tommy Taylor scored and there was a bloody big panic right up to the end!

"That was the last time the Queen and Duke presented the trophy. Eric Houghton had promised me that he'd take me to Ascot if we won. He kept his word and we were standing in the saddling enclosure when the Queen walked by. Eric and I bowed - and she smiled. 'You know, Nigger' said Eric 'she recognized you!!"

Sims had no time for his next manager, Joe Mercer. It seems that the feeling was mutual. Sims peeled back his summer shorts to show the remnants of a thigh wound which he bears as a constant reminder of one injury that Mercer made him play on with - "if you don't play, you'll never play again" said the manager.

"I had a cracking game one time at Old Trafford, but before the return match Mercer says to me "I've heard all about your off-field exploits. You just make sure you do your best for this team'. And I'd had a blinder the day before. He took us down to the Second Division - what with playing Stan Lynn at centre-forward and so on."

Fortunately, others had no doubts about the big man's attitude - or capabilities. Years before, Sims had played for the Army team. His brilliance at Villa Park brought him Football League recognition - at Leeds in October, 1957 and in Dublin three years later. On both occasions the League of Ireland were in opposition and victories of 3-1 and 4-0 ensued for Sims' team.

The side at Leeds read:

Sims: Jimmy Armfield (Blackpool); Ronnie Moran (Liverpool); Ray Barlow (West Brom); Jackie Charlton (Leeds); Reg Pearce (Luton); Albert Kaye (Barnsley); Peter Broadbent (Wolves, 1 goal); Ron Tindall (Chelsea); Ray Parry (Bolton, 2 goals); Peter Hooper (Bristol Rovers).

At Dalymount Park, only 'Nigger' remained:

Sims; John Sillett (Chelsea); Tony Allen (Stoke); Ronnie Clayton (Blackburn); Matt Woods (Blackburn); Mick McGrath (Blackburn); Peter Brabrook (Chelsea); Peter Dobing (Blackburn, 3 goals); Graham Moore (Cardiff); Jimmy Greaves (Chelsea, 1 goal); Frank Blunstone (Chelsea).

Nigel Sims played 244 League games for Villa. He also played in the first ever League Cup final ("That's a bloody waste of time - it's not worth tuppence 'alfpenny"), though was left out for the second leg against Rotherham, Geoff Sidebottom coming in. "And you won't even be in the team photo" Mercer told him. Sims had played in every game up to then.

Fortunately, Sims retained faith in his own ability, spurred on by the favourable comment invested in him by the immortal Frank Swift's regular News of the World columns. Years before, the boy Sims had thrilled to watch Swift in action against his own heroes, Derby County.

"Doherty, Carter, Woodley, Ward - and above all Leon Leuty. Years later I played for Young England against England and Leuty was on the other side! Marvellous. There was only one ground I yearned to play on - the Baseball Ground. And then I did, in the Second Divison for Villa and it was awful! It's so cramped and pokey - with those stands all around you, it's like playing in a tent!"

Swift and Bert Trautmann were Sims' idols. But without hesitation he lists Gordon Banks as the greatest of them all.

'He read the game well, took crosses well, was agile, had a good temperament...he had the lot. Mind you, there was one chap after me at the Wolves who had everything, too. I told him that if I'd had hold of him I'd have made him the best in the world. His build, stature, natural ability....those shoulders: you ask The Finn."

Paul Bradshaw proved a big disappointment to Sims. (So, too, incidentally, did Noel Dwyer, another custodian for whom he had high regard.) By joining Peterboro, Brad at least emulated the career of his more illustrious predecessor.

"Things got so bad at Villa I moved out after 9 years - another year and I'd have got a testimonial. But Mercer wanted rid and I couldn't stand to be under him any longer. I'd guested for Arsenal and a lot of clubs wanted me. But the chairman said I would never leave. Mercer kept pestering him, so I went to Canada and Toronto City on a free under Malcolm Allison. Come the end of the season in September I came back and both Peterborough and Swindon wanted me, but I signed for Gordon Clark at Peterborough on the agreement that I'd be released at the end of the season to go back to Canada. Later I played for Toronto Falcons and, in all, was there playing and coaching college kids for five years."

Since then, Nigel Sims has been a club-owner in Malvern, the Man from the Pru, and now makes mirrored wardrobes. His two sons live in Wolverhampton still, running an arborist business in Tettenhall.

"The eldest fancied being a keeper and had trials at Everton. But he didn't want it BADLY enough. You must if you're going to make it.

"Mind you, I've got so many aches and pains now that I wish I'd never bothered myself!"

A generation of Wolves and Villa supporters would never agree with that.

"MAN OF STEEL"

"Stan Cullis said I was the bravest keeper he'd known. Nigel Sims' retort to that was 'yeah - but that says nothing about skill!' You see, though, I had to be brave, if that's what I was. I simply wasn't as agile as the likes of Bert Williams."

Malcolm Finlayson knew full well that it would be no easy matter replacing Williams in the Wolves goal. Bert was a god in Wolverhampton and he had graced the Wanderers' goalmouth with aplomb for a dozen years of glorious success. That Wolves with Finlayson between the sticks proceeded to win the League twice and then the F.A.Cup in successive seasons as well as finish in the top three in one of the other two seasons for which he was senior choice, succinctly confirms the successful way in which Williams was replaced, irrespective of the new incumbent's different style.

Now, over thirty years since he first came to Wolverhampton, Malcolm Finlayson has proved himself as astute a businessman as he was courageous a keeper.

The board room of his hugely successful Kingswinford-based steel stockholding company is generously littered with photographs of past glories. There's Joe Gardiner's magic sponge reviving the burly Scot after a collision with Bryan Douglas in the 1960 Cup Final. Here's a cameo of Finlayson's steely nerve as he launches himself at the feet of rampaging Spur Bobby Smith. And, next to that, are line-ups of the magnificent League and Cup winning sides of the late fifties which made Wolverhampton Wanderers the pride of the Midlands. A neat pile of books about the Wolves lies in testimony to Malcolm Finlayson's continuing love affair with the club.

The tall Scot with that luxuriously mellow accent and Celtic good looks which don't seem to have changed over the passing years, cast his memory back to a childhood which began on the 14th June, 1930 at Alexandria, Dumbarton.

"I was always a goalkeeper, chiefly because I was marginally better there than outfield! What helped me enormously was that I played three games each Saturday as a 12-year-old. I'd play for the school team in the morning and then for the Boys Brigade Under-15's and Under-17's.

"My idol was Frank Swift. During the War he was guesting for Hamilton Academicals. I'd walk six yards behind him as he strolled to the ground from the station, never daring to talk to him. I admired him so much because he made the job look easy. Frank would position himself such that it seemed as if forwards were shooting straight at him. And he was so confident.

"I was playing myself a lot, so didn't get much chance to watch my local club Dumbarton. I do recall, however, going as an 11-year-old without permission to Hampden to watch Stan Cullis and his England team beat Scotland 4-0 in front of 150,000 people. They were so packed-in that I could lift my feet off the ground and not move an inch! I had no comprehension of the danger I was in - but I certainly got a hiding when I got home!

"I left school at fourteen to work in Denny's Shipyard in Dumbarton. At fifteen I played for Vale of Leven and also had three games for Dumbarton in the Scottish Second Division. They didn't sign me, so it was back to Vale of Leven before signing for Renfrew Juniors. As a sixteen-year-old I had three games for Celtic's reserve team, before going a year later to Millwall for a closed door trial match against Charlton. I was broken hearted that nobody in Scotland seemed to want me. In later years I discovered that both Leeds and Charlton (after that trial game) had fancied me joining them."

In February 1948, however, Malcolm Finlayson signed professional forms for Millwall, under the management of ex-England international Jack Cock.

"There were 48 professionals at The Den at the time and I became their sixth keeper! My first game was for the third team one snowy day against Leyton Orient when, with no goals scored, they abandoned things after twenty minutes. The first team, meanwhile, had lost 2-6 at home to Bury. Straightaway I was promoted to the Second Division team to play West Brom at The Den. We drew 2-2, a big improvement after a bad run, but we still finished bottom of the table.

"Millwall sacked Cock and installed Charlie Hewitt. He thought me too young and so signed Ted Hinton from Fulham, who at the time was Northern Ireland's keeper. He and I alternated for a couple of seasons, but in 1949/50 we finished bottom of Division 3(South). Nevertheless, we had a great bunch of lads and a super set of supporters, chiefly dockers. They were very loyal to the club and I, myself, was well-received."

Nevertheless, Malcolm Finlayson claims he didn't really learn anything at Millwall.

"It was frustrating being in the Third Division and not looking as if we were going anywhere. I wasn't an admirer of Hewitt's, neither were my colleagues. Years later, moving to Molineux was like a breath of fresh air: to come to work for a manager who was so straight."

One match above all the other 200-plus that Finlayson played for Millwall stands out for him.

"It was at Fellows Park. I got kicked in the face by Johnny Devlin and there was blood everywhere. Off I

went to hospital, but I was determined to get back to finish off the game. When we returned to the ground the gates were locked and they wouldn't let us in! The director that had accompanied me to hospital had to climb the gates to summon help! With my head in a bandage I trotted back onto the pitch, but to the goal I had vacated, not realising that they'd changed round at halftime! Jim Constantine, the former Manchester City player, had gone into goal and, by the time I returned, we were losing 3-1. A few minutes from the end it was 5-5 and then we scored again. Straight from the kick off, Walsall stormed down towards me and hit the bar!"

Just as fate had played a mysterious part in bringing Bert Williams and Nigel Sims to prominence, so too was Finlayson's route to Molineux paved in an unusual manner.

"I'd always been interested in doing somnething outside the game and, having just got married, I wanted to become a part-timer and find a second trade. I took courses and became a sales rep with Hartley's Jams, car supplied. My playing contract with Millwall finished on the 30th June, 1956 after a season in which we'd finished last again in Division 3(South) (goals for 83, goals against 100). The retain system at the time meant that even though I wouldn't sign a new contract, Millwall could hold on to my registration. At the time I was earning £20 in the season, £16 during the summer. Over at Charlton, Sam Bartram had just retired and Jimmy Seed, their manager, was prepared to let me do something outside the game if I joined as the replacement. The deal was just going through when Wolves' scout in the area (who owned a pub called The Valley!) told me that they were interested.

"I would have walked from London to play for Wolverhampton Wanderers. I talked to Stan Cullis, who agreed that I could do my spare-time stuff provided that it didn't interfere with my goalkeeping. So I signed - I believe the transfer fee was £2,500."

It was August 1956. Finlayson left Hartley's after some success and enrolled in Business Studies at Wolverhampton Technical College as well as becoming a rep for a steel stockholding company similar to the one he now masterminds.

"I carried on this routine until 1960 when I started my current company immediately after we'd won the cup. Dividing the time wasn't easy. I worked on a commission basis: it was football training in the morning, rep work in the afternoons, college in the evenings. I bought a small truck and used to pick up steel early in the morning, drive to Castlecroft for training, then deliver the stock in the afternoon. My wife did the invoices in the evenings on a typewriter which a customer sold to me for £1 10 shillings!"

Malcolm wasn't alone amongst the Wolves players in trying to ensure that he had another string to his bow.

"Roy Swinbourne worked as a rep for a tyre firm and became a big success. Bill Slater, of course, was a lecturer, whilst Bert Williams and Jimmy Mullen had their sports outfitter businesses. Eddie Stuart had a grocer's shop in Whitmore Reans.

"Players these days don't seem to make the same sort of provisions. There was, of course, less money from playing in those days. Even when we played the continental clubs the bonuses were poor. Nowadays you can take out insurance against the end of your career and so on. I had a much greater incentive to go out and work. Wolves were very strict: the League regulations said £20 maximum and that's what we got. There were no under-the-counter payments."

Malcolm Finlayson recalls his early playing days with Wolves as being not hugely successful in terms of his form.

"On the day I signed I watched Wolves' evening match with Luton at Molineux. It was the finest League game I ever saw, finishing 5-4 to Wolves. At one end was Bert Williams, the Big Cat. At the other end was Bernard Streten, only slightly less agile. These two made so many wonderful saves, I thought 'I can't follow this'. I really felt that way - I nearly went home!"

A little over a fortnight later, Finlayson's Division One baptism came in front of 40,824 spectators for the game with Leeds at home.

"It was a disaster. When John Charles outjumped me for a cross to head home it was the worst moment of my career. Then he switched from centre-forward to centre-half to thwart everything our forwards could throw at them."

Wolves lost 1-2 with a team reading:

Finlayson; Eddie Stuart; Bill Shorthouse; Bill Slater; Billy Wright; Ron Flowers; Harry Hooper; Peter Broadbent(1); Jimmy Murray; Denis Wilshaw; Jimmy Mullen.

Nevertheless, Finlayson kept his place for a dozen League games, as well as figuring in the floodlit friendly with Valencia and Wanderers' summer tour of South Africa.

"Unknown to me, Stan Cullis was reporting back to the Board of Directors and to secretary Jack Howley on whether he thought I would make the grade. Happily, he did.

"Yes, Bert Williams was a tough act to follow. He was hugely popular and the crowd didn't take to me at first. We had totally different styles. Bert could allow a fellow to hit the ball from seven or eight yards out he was tremendously agile. But I couldn't afford to let that happen. I used to go to get the ball at the opponent's feet. Alternatively I had to take advantage of angles, like Swift, and not be diving around all the time. The crowd didn't always appreciate what I was doing, but the people that matter did - in other words, Stan Cullis and the others behind the scenes.

"It was marvellous for me to know that Mr Cullis liked me: a man whom I admired and respected. Knowing that I had his confidence helped me to play better. That's why I felt so sorry recently for Lukic at Arsenal, him knowing that his manager was determined to get Seaman. What must that have done for his confidence?"

With Bert Williams retiring in 1957, Malcolm Finlayson returned from the club's South African jaunt as the senior keeper. He missed just five games in Wolves' Championship triumph of 1957-58, Eire international Noel Dwyer ably deputising. Wolves conceded fewer goals (47) than they had for eight seasons. A year later, as Wolves topped the pile again, just two extra goals were let in, and their Scottish keeper missed just three matches, giving a first chance to Geoff Sidebottom.

In spite of these exceptional club triumphs, representative honours passed the 6 foot Scot by.

"Yes, that was frustrating, particularly as Stan had recommended me and had been assured that I would be selected for Scotland in Wales. The cap never materialised. That I played for the greatest Wolves side ever, however, to my mind vindicated the situation. I had chances to go to a Scottish club, but frankly if it was a toss up between that improving my chances of a cap or playing for Wolves, I'd have chosen the latter every time."

And thus the big custodian had the opportunity to crown his Wolverhampton career with a cup winners medal in the 1960 triumph over Blackburn. And yet he could so easily have missed out.

"I'd played in the European Cup game in Barcelona and injured my shoulder in the 0-4 defeat. So I was out for a couple of months. When it came round to the F.A. Cup semi-final it was left to me whether I felt fit enough to play. Funnily, 'Nigger' Sims in the Villa goal was just as badly injured - we were both trying to cover up our wounds from the opposition.

Finlayson did play in the 1-0 triumph at The Hawthorns and went on to gain his precious medal in the uninspiring final. The fact that the Wembley occasion was an unspectacular affair is perhaps one of the reasons why Finlayson picks out the 3-2 triumph over Real Madrid in October, 1957 as being the highlight of his career. In that game one of Finlayson's characteristically hefty clearances was nodded on by Jimmy Murray for Peter Broadbent to notch the second goal.

Malcolm Finlayson's qualities as a goalkeeper were transparent, qualities for which he had much to thank the help at Millwall of 'Dusty' Miller and Jesse Carver, the coach imported from Juventus.

"Those two would coach me on a Sunday morning to rectify weaknesses that had shown up in my game the day before.

"At Wolves, Harry Potts (later to manage Burnley) and Joe Gardiner spent a lot of time with me, mostly in the afternoons when the others weren't training. When my turn came, I used to help Phil Parkes and Bob Wilson in a similar way."

Mention of subsequent Wolves keepers prompted the obvious question of which ones were rated most by Finlayson.

"Have there been any?!" came the tongue-in-cheek reply. "Seriously, I think that since the War only Bert Williams, myself and Phil Parkes ever really established themselves. Gary Pierce at Wembley in 1974 gave one of the finest displays of goalkeeping that I've ever seen, but for the most part I wasn't impressed by him. Paul Bradshaw? He could have been a great 'keeper.

"In my day I admired Bert Trautmann, even though he did let that one in at the near post in 1960 which allowed Burnley to win the League and stop us getting the double! Bartram, Ted Ditchburn, Bert of course, Jack Fairbrother, Jim Sanders - there were such a lot of good goalkeepers playing at the time. Yes, there are good ones today, of course there are. I like Woods, Shilton has been marvellous, Seaman, Lukic, too."

The shoulder injury suffered in Spain was proving troublesome to the Scot, so Sidebottom opened 1960-61. By February of that season, however, the Yorkshireman had followed Sims to Villa Park and manager Cullis brought in Chic Brodie.

"I felt sorry for Chic. The crowd didn't take to him and my injury healed faster than expected."

The following season, however, after a calamitous 7-2 defeat at Blackpool, Finlayson was deposed by the patient Fred Davies. A shock?

"Not really. I was devoting more and more time to my business. By now I was employing people. I was finding that customers wouldn't always wait for me to fit in my footballing. I told Stan that I was going to retire, but he asked me to stay on as a part-timer, training in the evenings. At the time I think we were on £40. I never discussed money with Stan, but when the contract came I found he'd only dropped me a nominal £3. That was really generous of him under the circumstances."

Finlayson played just one first team game in each of the next two seasons, ironically both at Anfield.

"In September 1963, Fred had been having a bad time so I was recalled. Roger Hunt hit a ball so hard that it smashed my hand and I had to come off. Jimmy Murray went into goal and we lost 6-0. I'm sure that if I hadn't been injured I'd have kept my place."

As it transpired, it was the loyal goalie's last fling in the senior side. The team makes nostalgic reading:

Finlayson; Bobby Thomson; Gerry Harris; John Kirkham; George Showell; Ron Flowers; Chris Crowe; Jimmy Murray; Ray Crawford; Peter Broadbent; Terry Wharton.

(It was Crawford's debut in the old gold - before the season had finished he himself had donned the keeper's sweater, substituting for the injured Davies at Bramall Lane.)

"My hand was smashed-up, making writing difficult. When I came back against West Brom Reserves, some big brawny lad kicked me on the knee, which put me into plaster for a few weeks. My wife had to drive me to my factory, then in Blackheath.

"Stan had said that if I found the business getting too much he'd release me. That's what he did. But he didn't cancel my contract - he paid me right up till the season's end. It was a wonderful gesture - typical of the man. Small wonder that I have great respect for him.

"He and I had our differences, of course we did. He was, as everybody knows, very hard. Everyone at some time or another had disagreements with him. I recall one time at Fulham when the ball was crossed over at knee height. Our right winger, who shall remain nameless(!) had only to stab it home, but saw tough old Jim Langley approaching. So that was that - he chickened out! At half time, Stan walked in, glanced at the winger and simply said 'I wouldn't want to be with you in the trenches!'."

To this day, Stan Cullis and Malcolm Finlayson remain firm friends, with the latter driving his former manager to Wembley for most of the internationals. Meanwhile, Finlayson retained his allegiance to the old gold long after playing.

"I was a season ticket holder from 1964 to 1983, when the Bhattis took over. I was a shareholder, too, from the early sixties until receivership."

And, of course, the name Finlayson loomed large in 1982 when Wolverhampton Wanderers had their first brush with disaster. In the first attempt at a rescue, Doug Ellis was installed as chairman with Malcolm Finlayson as vice chairman. They lasted three weeks.

"Even before that I'd twice been voted onto the Board by the shareholders and twice voted off it by Harry Marshall. There aren't many people to have been a director of Wolves on three occasions for such brief periods of time!"

It became clear, however, that the Receivers would not entertain the Ellis-Finlayson package. Dougan brought in the Bhattis and four years of calamitous history ensued.

"It is marvellous that the club has been saved and that the council took over the ground the way they did. I now wish that something would happen to put the place back together. When the Waterloo Road stand re-opens, I'll get my season ticket again!"

THE TWELFTH MAN

There are players who have little, if any, recall of the games they played in their careers. Some, though, seem to have the ability for total recollection. I'm unclear whether there is any link between this and the love which a man has for the sport. If such is the case, however, there can be fewer players with a greater appreciation of football than Geoff Sidebottom, veteran of just 35 first team appearances for Wolverhampton Wanderers but a man whose robust Yorkshire tones speak to this day with great affection about his life and times behind the gold and black.

Geoff Sidebottom was born at Mapplewell, near Barnsley, on 29th December, 1936. He discovered a natural leaning towards goalkeeping at an early age.

"I was always a keeper at Darton Hall school. In fact in my first year I played for all three teams at the various age levels."

Sidebottom's abilities fetched him a place in the Barnsley Schoolboys side, yet he was not especially committed to the game, packing in playing on leaving school.

"I went to work in a foundry at 15. Then the goalie from the village side went off for a trial (unsuccessful!) to Blackpool and I was asked to play."

Geoff caught the attention of the scouts and was invited by Mark Crook to join the Wolves' nursery side at Wath-upon-Dearne.

"I used to play for Wath in the Northern Intermediate League on a Saturday morning. Mark Crook, though, also used to run a side in a Sheffield league on a Saturday afternoon and I would play centre-forward for them, against works sides and the like.

"I didn't have that many games for Wath because mostly I travelled down to Wolverhampton to play for the third or fourth teams and the F.A. Youth Cup side."

The 17-year-old Yorkshireman came into the Youth side halfway through the 1953-54 campaign for the 1-0 victory at Nottingham Forest. Thereafter, wins over Portsmouth and West Ham carried the young Wolves side into the two-legged final against the doyens of youth soccer, Matt Busby's Manchester United.

"I have big memories of that final. They had a fine team, with the likes of Duncan Edwards, Bobby Charlton, David Pegg and Albert Scanlon. We had large gates for both games - in fact, I think they presented the League Championship trophy to Wolves at the Molineux match."

That leg was drawn 4-4, with United squeezing through 1-0 at Old Trafford via a penalty. Wolves fielded

Sidebottom; Griffiths; Harris; Bolton; Timmins; Fallon; Round; Mason; Bonson; Murray; Cooper.

Geoff Sidebottom knew Joe Bonson well from their days together with Barnsley Boys. In his time at Molineux, Geoff recalls Ted Farmer, Phil Kelly and, especially, Harry Middleton as close friends.

"Wolves wanted me to join the groundstaff, but I kept travelling. I signed pro in September 1954 and moved into Jimmy Murray's old digs in Fordhouses. Gwyn Jones lived up the road."

The young keeper patiently learned his trade in the Wanderers' junior and reserve sides, carefully watching Bert Williams, Nigel Sims, 'Paddy' Dwyer and Malcolm Finlayson.

"Bert was brilliant - he'd help you so much with extra sessions in the afternoon and the like. Dwyer was a good keeper, too - a bit hot-headed of course. But then there were other young 'uns coming through, too, such as 'Paddy' Cullen and Fred Davies. I got on well with Fred."

Geoff Sidebottom also had a lot of respect for his manager.

"Stan Cullis was an honest fellow. You can't wish for anything better in a manager. If you went to ask for something and he said you could have it, then you'd have it. If he said no then you knew he meant no."

"My biggest problem to start with was a lack of confidence - I'm basically a shy person. I was 17, I'd met Bert Williams and I didn't see how I could be at the same place as such a marvellous keeper.

"People used to say that my strongest point was my bravery. Honestly, I never used to think about getting injured. I vowed to myself that if ever I hesitated through fear of getting hurt, then I'd jack it in. To me, I was just average."

Average or not, it was only a question of time before the up-and-coming keeper would get a first team chance. In fact it came four years after signing professional forms. Williams had retired; Sims had moved on; Finlayson was injured; and Noel Dwyer was out of favour.

"There had been rumours all week that Finlayson wasn't going to make it and that it was a toss-up between me and Noel. I'd been playing in the Central League in place of Noel. On the Friday Mr Cullis called me in to tell me that he was choosing me."

The occasion could hardly have been more feverous: a local derby at The Hawthorns in front of 48,898 spectators.

"I was a bundle of nerves, but the first thing that Billy Wright did was to pass the ball back to give me a feel. After that I was fine - I didn't even notice the crowd. Bobby Robson and Ronnie Allen were in their team, and Fred Potter was in goal. He'd only played a couple of games himself. I did alright - in fact we lost to a back pass in the last minute. Eddie Stuart's ball fell short and Derek Kevan nipped in."

Wolves' team which succumbed 1-2 read
Sidebottom; Stuart; Gerry Harris; Bill Slater; Wright; Ron Flowers; Norman Deeley (1); Peter Broadbent; George Showell; Bobby Mason; Jimmy Mullen.

Sidebottom retained his place for First Division victories over Preston and at Burnley, as well as for the 2-2 draw with Schalke 04 in the first leg of the European Cup tie.

"I thought I did alright and was a bit surprised to be left out, but you make the best of it."

It was just as well that Sidebottom was of a philosophical disposition, for what happened in the following season would have broken the spirit of many a player. On February 10, Malcolm Finlayson hurt his shoulder in Barcelona, leaving an opening for the eager Sidebottom. Apart from a run of six League games, of which only one was lost, the 23-year-old reserve figured in the return encounter with the Spanish champions at Molineux as well as the fifth and sixth round F.A. Cup triumphs over Luton and Leicester respectively.

"A week after we'd beaten Leicester in the Cup, we lost 1-2 to them in the League, also at Filbert Street. I hadn't had a bad game - but Stan left me out for the semi-final the following Saturday. He was on about it being 'because of the occasion'. I was very, very disappointed. In fact I was made twelfth man in the semi. But in my pocket was a transfer request. One of the senior players said to me 'take it with you by all means and give it to Stan if we lose. But if we win, tear it up because you don't know what's going to happen'.

"We won of course - and four days later I was back in for the visit of Burnley, who went on to win the League. We won 6-1, yet they murdered us. Every week after that until the end of the season I was twelfth man."

At the start of 1960-61, Geoff Sidebottom got another opportunity.

"Malcolm and I BOTH got carried off during the annual Coloureds against Whites public practice match! I got in for the Charity Shield match at Burnley the following week - it poured down! Then the first League game was against West Ham, who unveiled 4-2-4. We ran around for twenty minutes not knowing what had hit us!

"As soon as Malcolm got fit again he came back, but he got lolloped two or three times so I was brought in once more. Then I got injured at West Ham. They thought I'd broken my leg, but Bobby Moore's plastic studs had severed the nerves just under my knee. I've still got the scar."

It was December 17th, Wolves went on to lose 0-5 and the name Sidebottom was never pencilled onto a Wolves senior team sheet again. In February, 1961 he was transferred to Aston Villa for £15,000, at the time the third highest fee ever paid for a goalkeeper.

"I had a phone call on the Saturday morning to go to the ground because Joe Mercer was waiting. I was happy in the Midlands so I was content to go to Villa. It turned out to be the worst move I ever made. I never got on with Joe Mercer. I was really unhappy."

In fact Geoff stayed four seasons at Villa Park, travelling from his Wolverhampton home with former Molineux colleagues Bobby Thomson and rival for the keeper's jersey, Nigel Sims. A League Cup winners' tankard was insufficient compensation for the frustrations he was suffering.

"One time Dougan, Thomson and I were put on the transfer list for daring to question the tactics. Clubs came in for me, I knew for a fact. Dick Taylor, Mercer's assistant, confirmed that there had been interest. But Mercer insisted that he'd heard nothing. It reached the stage where I came to watch a game at Wolves and the press lads were telling me that I was due to sign for Northampton the next day!

"One Sunday in January 1965 my closest friend and roommate, Phil Woosnam, called me up to say that Scunthorpe were interested. By that time I'd have gone to Timbuctoo to get away!"

In fact, Geoff enjoyed greatly his stint at the Old Show Ground, giving him as it did the opportunity to work for the first time under Freddie Goodwin - "a hell of a great bloke, so honest".

Understudy to Sidebottom for Scunthorpe's highly-placed Third Division side was a skinny gentleman, like Geoff of 5 feet 10 inches, by the name of Raymond Clemence.

"Ray was a funny boy - they were going to let him go to Skeggy (Skegness). He was a dangly lad, so lazy in training. Yet when I saw him in games he always looked good. They had another lad called Alan Wilson who never looked like he was going to be a goalkeeper, but either him or Ray was going to be got rid of. I gave them my opinion and Ray stayed on. When I got a kick in the kidneys they brought him in - I think they got walloped seven at Grimsby. But he looked good. I'd take him under the old stand and knock hell out of him. But it was the only way to get him working. You had to get under his skin. I remember our trainer saying 'you'll kill the bloody lad'!"

Geoff Sidebottom, though, was sowing the seeds for a great goalkeeper of the future. Clemence's emergence allowed the Lincolnshire club to release their senior man, who followed Freddie Goodwin to New York Generals.

"I was there for two years with the likes of George Kirby, Micky Ash and Barrie Wright. Cesar Menotti was in the squad - but wasn't a regular starter. We called him 'Cannonball' after he once nigh on hit a penalty right out of the ground!

"It was brilliant out there. I used to coach at Columbia University. They wanted me to stay on fulltime, but I came back with Freddie to Brighton. I really should have stayed - but Brighton was probably the best club I've ever been to for the set of lads. It was so homely: Alex Dawson, Nobby Lawton, Willie Bell. Norman Wisdom was on the Board."

Sadly, Geoff had to abandon playing in 1970-71.

"I'd had a lot of bangs on the head. The first had been in my first ever Friday match for Villa at Everton. I spent the Saturday night in a Liverpool hospital. I still have the photo of Alex Young making contact with me. Then I had another in America and a couple more at the Goldstone. I was sent to see Roger Bannister who said that if I had another he wouldn't be responsible: I could be killed or else end up a cabbage."

And so it was back up to Scunthorpe where for ten years now he has happily worked for a company manufacturing international railway parts. In fact Geoff works a 60 foot plane, the only one of its kind in the world. He watches little soccer.

"I used to be a regular at Scunthorpe, but results seem to be everything now whereas it's entertainment that should matter. Bang! Chase that! No thanks - I'd sooner watch local football."

Geoff also bemoans the shortage of class goalkeepers these days.

"Peter Shilton of course is fantastic for his age. But I don't reckon there's much about at the moment. There used to be a glut. Coton is about the best of the bunch.

"I admired Gordon Banks - I recall playing against Chesterfield Reserves at Molineux when we did them nine, but Banksy had a blinder!

"But above all I admired Bert Williams, as a goalkeeper and as a person. Nothing was ever too much trouble. He's one of the nicest blokes I've ever met inside or outside football."

THE MAN WITH THE KNOWLEDGE

Next time you're in 'The Smoke' and your taxi-driver looks a wee bit familiar, listen to him carefully. Should he speak with a Scottish lilt and if the conversation drifts in the general direction of football, then you might just have stumbled upon Chic Brodie. Even so, it's much more likely that you'll recognize him if you're a fan of Aldershot or Brentford. Even longer-term Wolves supporters might be excused for 'missing' him, for he spent precious little time as a Wanderer.

Charles Brodie (he has been 'Chic' from being a youngster) was born in Duntocher, near Loch Lomond on 22nd February 1937. He was always a goalkeeper.

"I won five caps for Scotland Schoolboys in the early fifties, alongside the likes of Ralph Brand, George Thomson and Ronnie Yeats. Three of those games were against England. We lost 0-1 at Wembley, 1-4 at Aberdeen and then drew one each at Love Street. Those are great memories -Duncan Edwards was captain of England.

"I ardently supported Glasgow Rangers - I still do! Yet I signed pro for Manchester City in March 1954. The senior keeper was Bert Trautmann who taught me such a lot. He was one helluva nice man. Even so I managed just one first team game for City, a friendly against Blackpool."

And so, in July 1957, Brodie, suitably educated by the great German, had signed for Gillingham, for whom he played 19 League games.

"I had been a part-timer at Maine Road. My old man wanted me to get a trade, so I took an electrical apprenticeship with Metropolitan Vickers at Trafford Park. Because of this my National Service was deferred until I was 21, when I joined up with the Royal Army Medical Corps at Aldershot for two years. I got into the British Army team alongside Chris Crowe, John Smith, Alex Young, Davie Wilson, Budgie Byrne and John Barnwell. As a Third Division player that was quite a feather in my cap."

Brodie had signed in July 1958 for the local club at the Recreation Ground and, in all, he played 95 League games for Aldershot.

"A number of managers were supposed to be watching me whilst I was playing for the Army team."

Amongst those managers was Stanley Cullis, but the great man had the opportunity of seeing young Brodie much closer to home.

"Aldershot had drawn a cup-tie at Stoke and the replay finished all-square, too. The second replay in those days was on a neutral ground, in this case Molineux. Things went well for me and I signed for Wolves the next day."

It was February, 1961. The fee was £14,000, just under that paid by Villa in the same month for the services of Geoff Sidebottom.

"My wife was expecting and our house down South was just ready for us to move into, so we never did move to the Midlands. I went into digs with Terry Wharton and David Woodfield.

"Malcolm Finlayson was injured, so I was thrilled to get my chance straightaway against Manchester United at Molineux, who included my old friend Bobby Charlton, against whom I'd played so many times at junior and reserve level in Manchester."

Wolves won 2-1, fielding
Brodie; Eddie Stuart; George Showell; Eddie Clamp; Bill Slater; John Kirkham; Norman Deeley; Ron Flowers (1); Ted Farmer; Peter Broadbent; Cliff Durandt. (The other Wolves scorer was Shay Brennan, own goal.)

38,526 people were on hand to see a unique game: Chic Brodie's first and last as the Wolverhampton Wanderers first team keeper.

"The next match was at Tottenham. Finlayson was fit again and came straight back. I never got another look-in. I was sick, choked."

Chic Brodie had to make do with second and third team football and watch in frustration as Wolves were dispatched from the European Cup Winners Cup by his old favourites, the Light Blues from Ibrox (matches recalled by Malcolm Finlayson as the greatest disappointment of his Molineux career).

Seven unhappy months after his arriving in Wolverhampton, a £6,000 transfer fee took Brodie to Northampton Town.

"The best memories of my career are of my time at the County Ground. It's a nice little town, the club was very friendly and we had a great bunch of lads. We won the Third Division in 1963 and, all told, I had 87 League games for them. Then I got tonsilitis and lost my place. Good luck to the lad who came in (Brian Harvey), but I never got back.

"I was on my way again in November, 1963. It was going to be either Brentford or Norwich and, of course, I chose the former. We had a lot of good young players and Jack Dunnett, chairman at the time, spent a lot of money. We just kept missing out on promotion and even in the year QPR walked the division we did them six-one."

Brodie spent eight seasons at Griffin Park, featuring in 201 League games.

"Then it was to Margate in the Southern League for a couple of seasons under Gerry Baker. But I got sick of the travelling from my London home. After a brief spell with Wealdstone I got fed up with the game and that was that."

By now, Chic was throwing himself into his new life as a London cabbie.

"My buddy Pat Terry put me on to it at Northampton. He told me that if ever I was in London I should do 'the knowledge'. So I did - twenty years ago when I was at Brentford. You go out on your moped, get a Blue Book off the Public Carriage Offce, and learn the routes. It's hard - don't do it! There's a lot of studying, a lot of learning parrot-fashion. You must sit tests. It took me eighteen months.

"Nowadays I cover the whole of London, so I've a full (green) badge. Mickey Block - he done the knowledge, too. You meet lots of interesting people - I picked up Geoff Hurst, Bobby Moore....Budgie Byrne!

"I swap about, days and evenings. The bloody traffic is terrible - it's good to do evenings to get away from the worst of the traffic. I'm my own boss and can start and finish when I please."

Think on, then - if your taxi-driver is unmistakably Scottish, see if it's Chic Brodie. I'm sure he'll be delighted to reminisce with you.

THE YOUNG CAT

"He is such a nice man!"

If I've heard that said once about Fred Davies, I've heard it said a hundred times. It's true, too! There can't be many more-well-thought-of chaps in the game today. To meet him in the flesh over a steaming cuppa at the Hilton Park Services during the Summer of 1990 was a pleasure. He puffed contentedly on a formidable cigar, as we trod back through the years over the ups and downs of a peripatetic career.

Fred Davies was born on the 22nd August 1939. The distinct traces of Scouse which decorate his voice sing out in testimony to his Little Woolton Street birthplace, a mile from the centre of Liverpool.

"I went to Harrison Jones' school, where the highlight for me would be when I had a chance to play in goal, but they used to play me at centre-forward. I played one cup-final at Goodison up front, which was great as I was an Evertonian. Later on I had a trial for the club, but didn't hear anything afterwards.

"I left school at 15 to work with Levis, a glass-cutting firm in the city, before joining Dysons, the trailer-making company. I played goal for a team in a Liverpool men's league and we'd lose by sevens and eights and I'd get knocked all over the place. But it was good grounding. There wasn't much in the way of facilities in those days: I actually trained in the same gym as the likes of the famous boxers Dick Tiger, Sam Longford and so on.

Fred Davies soon joined Borough United, the Welsh club which within a few years would earn European recognition after winning the Welsh Cup.

"A fellow called Tommy Lane used to collect about seven of us in a van outside the entrance to the Mersey Tunnel and take us over to Llandudno Junction. There was something in the boot for travelling! After three quarters of a season, Alf Hanson, brother of the old Bolton 'keeper and a Wolves scout, approached me. Did I want a trial? When I told dad, a Liverpool docker, he was like a dog with two.....we couldn't keep him still! When he and mum came down to meet Mr Cullis he was thrilled."

Young Fred signed for Wolves in the April after his seventeenth birthday. It was as a full professional -he was too old for an apprenticeship.

"Stan, though, made me come down that summer and work on the ground just as an apprentice would to get me used to the digs. I was so homesick and couldn't wait to get home at the weekend. Once I travelled up with an old Wolves keeper whose name escapes me and it was he that convinced me that I should persevere - that it would all be worthwhile if and when I made the grade."

Davies started at Molineux as sixth choice keeper. Being a touch older than the other lads, too, meant that he didn't quite qualify for the F.A. Youth Cup side that took the trophy in dramatic style after a 6-5 aggregate win over Chelsea. Johnny Cullen had that privilige.

"In that first year my fitness improved greatly. I was playing in the fourth team in the Worcestershire Combination. But then I couldn't see myself getting anywhere. So I went to Bert Williams' shop and asked his advice. Would he look at me? Bert came to Castlecroft and did just that. Our friendship built up. Afternoons, after training, I would work in his shop, drive his van, do anything to help. And then every Monday he'd pick me up from Molineux with a bag of balls and off we'd go to Castlecroft. The help and guidance which Bert gave me was invaluable. He'd watch me in matches and afterwards we'd analyse what I'd done, how I might have done things differently."

So did Fred model himself on the legendary former England star?

"I suppose so, yes, in that I believed in a lot of what Bert did. They'd call me The Young Cat! I suppose I was agile and a good shot stopper: I was so confident in my angles. All that came from Bert."

National Service was just finishing for the young men of the country, but Fred Davies was one of the last to be called up - for the RAF at Bridgnorth, alongside Ron Atkinson.

"I told the Chief Scout George Noakes that they were posting me to Catterick and he had a word in the right ear, such that I went instead to Compton Bassett to train as a telephonist! Then I got posted back to Bridgnorth. I played for the RAF as well as the Wolves when I could, but I also had to turn out for the camp. So I told them I'd like to play out for fitness' sake - I got 53 goals one season!"

Back in goal, Fred graduated to Wolves' Central League side around the time that the seniors had won through to the 1960 F.A. Cup final.

"John Harris, the fullback, and I took our girlfriends (Maureen is now my wife) down for the game in John's Morris Minor. The car blew up on the motorway and we were towed off into Dunstable. We managed to find a double room in a hotel for the girls but had to persuade a policeman to put John and I up for the night in a cell! We drove to Wembley the next day on a reconditioned engine!"

The eager young keeper finally got his first senior chance after almost five years patient slog through the reserves and juniors. A week after a 7-2 debacle at Blackpool in January 1962, Wolves had a fourth round cup-tie at Molineux against their old rivals from West Bromwich. Phil Kelly and George Showell stepped aside to enable Bobby Thomson and Fred Goodwin to make their debuts. And in goal Malcolm Finlayson was replaced by Davies.

Fred Davies: Eddie Stuart; Bobby Thomson; Fred Goodwin; Bill Slater; Ron Flowers; Terry Wharton; Jimmy Murray(1); Barry Stobart; Peter Broadbent; Cliff Durandt.

"As you ran out, your hair stood on end: there were over 46-thousand in the ground."

Regrettably Davies' best endeavours couldn't keep the Baggies at bay and Wolves were knocked out of the cup by two goals to one. The 22-year-old custodian, however, had done enough to earn his place in the side and for the next two seasons he was undisputed first choice. He had convinced Stanley Cullis that he was worth the nod over Finlayson.

"To me Stan Cullis was brilliant. He was very hard, but he was very straight. Those steel horseshoes on his heels! When he walked down the corridor you certainly knew he was coming! If Jack Davies had put out his white tracksuit then look out! Stan was coming training.

"When I told Stan that I was getting married and that I would like a club house, he tried to talk me out of it. 'A young lad like you - why get married?!' Anyway, we went looking for flats and he called me in. 'Are you still going through with this wedding of yours?' he asked. 'Yes' I replied 'I'm looking for properties'. 'Yes, I know!' said Stan 'go and have a look at this' and he handed me a bunch of keys. It was a semi at Penn, which we bought eventually. That was typical of Stan - he did an awful lot of checking out; he'd help any way he could."

Fred and Maureen were married 31 years ago. They now have two daughters, Gaynor Marie (26) and Lindsey Siân (23). Bobby Mason was next door neighbour, but Fred also counted Johnny and Gerry Harris and Ted Farmer as his friends. ("Ted will give you a different view on Stan Cullis, but I always tell him that it's how you find people.")

"But you were friendly with an awful lot - Alan Hinton, Terry Wharton, 'Slipper' Read - it was a close club in that sense. There were no cliques in those days."

1962-1963, despite one of the worst winters for weather ever, was a season of some success at Molineux, starting with a spectacular 8-1 victory for Cullis' young wolf cubs over Manchester City, Bert Trautmann included. The following season, though, was lacklustre and, after a dismal start to 1964-1965, Stanley Cullis was astonishingly dismissed.

"That was a tremendous shock for the younger players. Andy Beattie came in.....aye!"

Fred Davies sighs and shakes his head.

"I'll always remember New Year's Day in January, 1965. It was a Friday night. The team sheet had gone up for the game at Highbury and I was on it. I was all set to catch the train to London with the rest of the lads next morning. The 'phone rang - it was Beattie. 'I've bought Dave Maclaren' he tells me. 'Where does that leave me?' I ask. 'You play in the Reserves tomorrow against Leeds', he says. 'And where does that leave the young lad (Phil Parkes) whose been chosen for that team?' I asked. So although I'd originally been selected for the first team, I ended up playing in the fourth team on the Saturday morning!"

Wolves lost 4-1 to the Arsenal and, with Maclaren being cuptied after his £8,000 transfer from Plymouth Argyle, Davies was back in the line-up a week later for the Third Round of the F.A. Cup at Portsmouth. He stayed in the side throughout a valiant cup run which ended in a 5-3 defeat against Manchester United at Molineux.

"Denis Law was magnificent that day. I remember lining the wall up at the Cow Shed end and he bent the ruddy thing right round it as I flew across - no chance!"

After a 7-4 reverse at White Hart Lane, Maclaren snatched his place back and retained it through the start of Wolves' first season in Division Two for 33 years in 1965-1966. On September 18th they lost 9-3 at Southampton.

"And Beattie dropped just George Miller and Bobby Woodruff. I was flabbergasted. But, then, we'd gone from having a manager in Cullis who you could trust to a situation where there were people that lied to you.

"Nevertheless I still respect the club - after eleven years there you don't lose that affinity. And I still watch games there when I can - it's great to see them doing well: Wolves are a first division club."

Beattie departing, the club went under the control of coach Ronnie Allen - "who didn't rate me" says Davies. An injury to Maclaren, though, forced Allen to play Fred in eight successive matches.

"We opened Bristol City's new lights just after Christmas in 1965, before taking the next day off. On the Thursday Ronnie Allen called me in to tell me that he was leaving me out. 'The chairman doesn't like you'. I told him that I simply didn't believe that as John Ireland had never indicated as much. I asked to see Mr Ireland and, in front of him, Allen denied that he'd ever said such a thing.

"Next he tried to get me off to Swindon and I met up with their manager Danny Williams. He came up to Molineux to see Allen and afterwards warned me that Allen was threatening to play me with the kids. Allen was asserting that I was asking for the town hall steps. I wasn't - I simply felt that it wasn't the right move for me.

"So, from having been the first team goalkeeper on the Monday, I was training on the park and playing in the fourth team with the kids. It was hard playing with the triallists and trying to help the youngsters along. But goalkeeping is goalkeeping at any level and Allen wasn't going to beat me. Week after week the trainer would show me the reports he had written: they proved how hard I'd been working.

"This went on for a while. Then Allen phoned me. 'I'm going into a board meeting. Dave Maclaren has broken a bone in his foot. I just want to make sure that you'll try if I put you into the team'! It's unprintable what I said to him."

Davies re-secured his first team spot in the second game of the promotion season 1966-1967, Maclaren soon afterwards moving on, ironically, to Southampton. In February 1967 after a 3-1 Fourth Round F.A. Cup tie defeat at the hands of Fred's old heroes at Goodison Park, Ronnie Allen gave Phil Parkes his chance, and the loyal Liverpudlian, by now on the transfer list, was to play just two more games for Wolves, the next season when Parkes had been suspended.

"We lost at Spurs 2-1 and then again to Leicester 3-1 at Molineux. Allen came into the dressing room, going on about his plans. I stood up and said 'I hope you're not including me - I obviously don't fit in with them'."

Despite Ronnie Allen's reservations about Evan Williams, the young Scot was made second choice keeper and Fred Davies was once more consigned to the obscurities of junior soccer. In January 1968 he signed for Second Division Cardiff at a fee of £12,000. He could look back on a totally loyal career at Molineux of 173 senior games. Fred had also been summoned for England Under-23 training but injury had given Birmingham's Colin Withers the chance instead, much to Davies' frustration. And on August 28th 1967, Fred had also reminded Wolves' fans of his capabilities as an outfield player.

"The 'B' team keeper Phil Weir was the substitute for the Central League team against Bury at Molineux. He came on and I went up front. I recall big Alex Dawson, against whom I'd had some great clashes when he played for United and Preston, saying to me 'Fred, what on earth are you doing up here? Don't bother coming over the halfway line!' Over came a corner and I got in behind Alex and scored. He didn't half give me some bruises after that!"

The Wolves team winning 2-0 that night makes nostalgic reading:

Fred Davies (1); Stewart Ross; Glen Andrews; Graham Hawkins; David Galvin; John McAlle; Peter Knowles; Brian Thompson; Alun Evans (1); John Farrington; Paddy Buckley.

Five months later Fred Davies was based at Ninian Park.

"They were in relegation trouble at the time but we pulled clear. Those were very happy times - I never wanted to leave and it was a big disappointment when Cardiff sold me to Bournemouth. I think they thought I was getting too old at 31. John Bond signed me - he was rebuilding his team. Probably that was the hardest thing I've ever been asked to do. Bournemouth had just sold David Best to Ipswich. He was the local lad for whom the fans had such affinity. But I had a tremendous few years, learning such a lot about the game from John Bond, who's a brilliant coach. I have an enormous amount of respect for him. We had a really fit team - John allowed us to express ourselves. He wanted me to do all the goalkeeping in the club. I felt I helped Keiron Baker, and we had Ron Tilsed the youth international who was farmed off everywhere (including to the Wolves): I think they wanted the money for him."

Keiron Baker took over from Davies, after Fred had taken a nasty knock at Rochdale.

"At first I had pins and needles in my fingers and toes. The hospital stuck me in a collar for 6 weeks, before a specialist told me how lucky I'd been. A vertebra had trapped a nerve - had the nerve snapped I'd have been a cripple."

Fred got back to the reserves but, after long consideration, decided to bring his playing days to an end and join John Bond at Norwich, in charge of the reserves. Next it was back to Dean Court as assistant to John Benson "which was probably a mistake because of the hassle there had been when I'd left for Norwich - they said it had been an illegal approach job. Alec Stock took over and, in his wisdom, duly disbanded the reserve and youth sides, which we'd had going really well. We had a lad called Roberts, for instance, at centre-forward. So he had to go - to Dorchester and then to Weymouth, before Spurs picked him up. You know the rest - it was Graham Roberts."

Next stop was Blackpool, looking after Alan Ball's youth team. But, after Ball's departure for The Dell as a player, Davies got disillusioned and took a pub near Merthyr Tydfil.

"Merthyr asked me to take over there, which I did for six months and they've gone on to do well under my successor. But I couldn't cope with being answerable to a committee and resigned. John Bond rang. He'd asked me to go with him to Burnley and Manchester City. Now he wanted me to join him at Swansea. So I went back to doing what I enjoyed best. Tommy Hutchinson took over and then the receivers came in and it was the first time ever that I'd been interviewed for my own job! 'I hear that you are essential to the workings of this club' was what the receiver said - and stuck me on a weekly contract. John Bond called again, this time from St Andrews and I went up as Assistant Manager four years ago. I looked after everything beneath the first team - and was thrilled to have a dozen lads go through to play first team football. At Birmingham I got some great help from Brian Caswell, Mick Murray, John Halford and Stuart Masefield, who did a tremendous job." A few months after we had met up John Bond had called again, to take Fred to Shrewsbury Town as his Assistant.

Fred Davies, of course, takes much interest in his young keepers and stresses how keepers are always insistent that they need the extra practice - hence the growth industry in goalkeeper coaches. Fred himself has done a lot of keeper coaching, including course work at Lilleshall alongside the likes of Mike Kelly, Alan Hodgkinson, John Osborne and Gordon Banks.

"Mick Kearns was the lad who came from the Wolves - he said then that if he'd learned as a youngster the sort of things we were going through then he'd have been a much better 'keeper."

Fred Davies rated highly Gordon Banks, Gordon West of Everton and Peter Bonetti and, perhaps surprisingly, Gary Bailey, who he expected to be England's keeper had injury not cruelly intervened. David Beasant and Kevin Hitchcock also impressed when he saw them at close quarters on coaching courses.

For my part, Fred Davies was a boyhood hero. There are some heroes that never fail to disappoint when you meet them in the flesh. Fred Davies certainly isn't one of those. He really is a genuinely nice man.

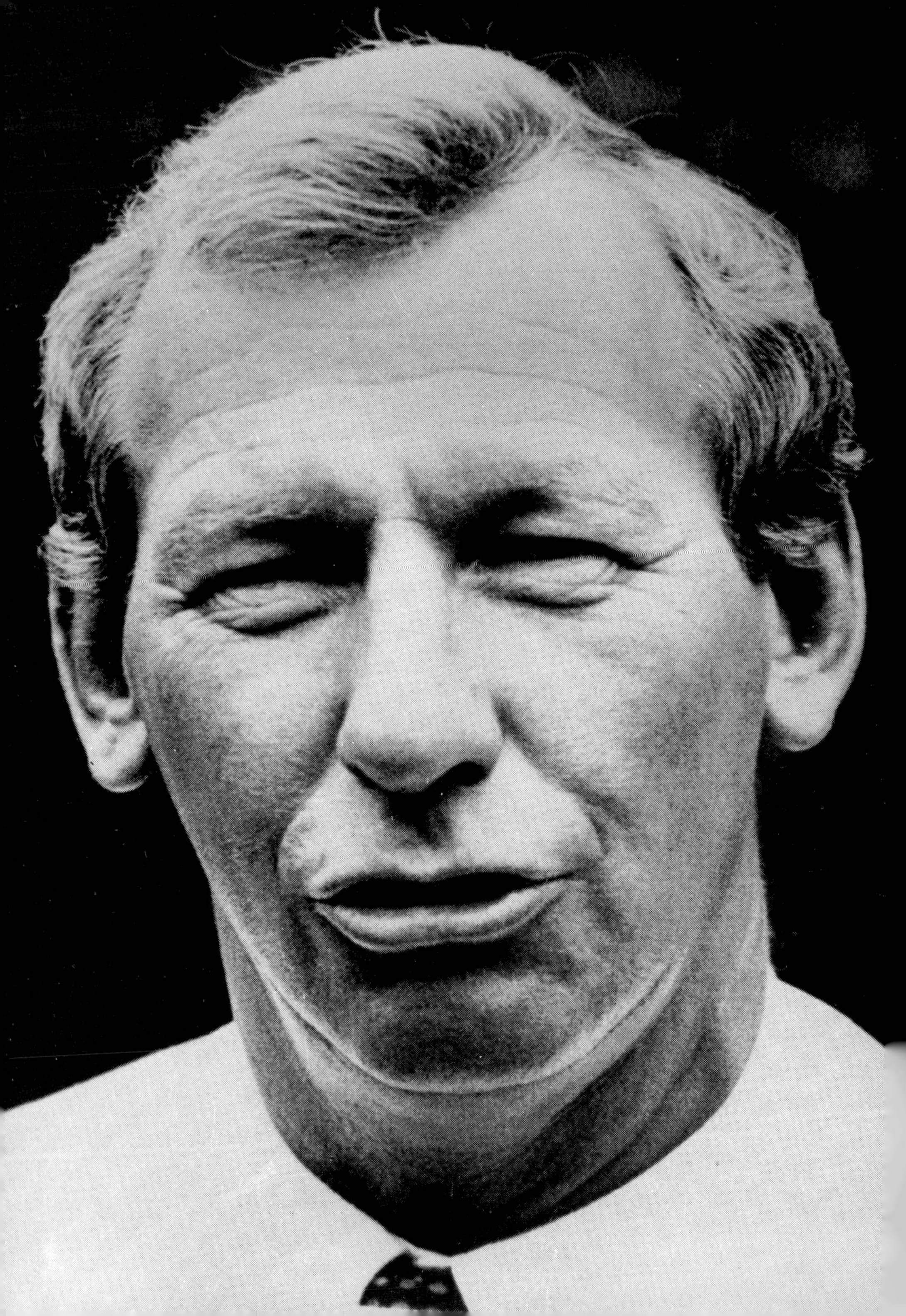

BEFORE THE GRANDSTAND

'You've Got To Be Crazy' is the title of Bob Wilson's splendid treatise on the world's goalkeeping greats. As for himself, the famous television personality is living testimony to the fact that the intelligensia, too, can make pretty fair custodians.

Bob Wilson was born in Chesterfield on 30th October 1941, the youngest of six children; Mum and Dad were Scottish.

"I was brought up very much as a Scot - I had a kilt as a child! I felt Scottish, even with the Chesterfield accent.

"As a youngster I quickly got fanatical about goalkeeping. After all, they do say that all you have to do in Chesterfield is shout down at the pit head and they'll send up a keeper! There'd been Sam Hardy and Ray Middleton, for instance. Ray, who played for England 'B', was one of my mentors - he sat as a J.P. on the same bench as my mum. Banksy, of course, was born in Sheffield, but played his early football for Chesterfield. I saw him play his first League game for the club - and, of course, played against him years later. And then there was John Osborne who went on to play for West Brom - he was left half in the town schoolboy side for which I kept goal!

"When I was a lad, Ronnie Powell was the Spireites' keeper. He'd been reserve at Manchester City to my idol: Bert Trautmann. I seized every opportunity to watch Bert in action. Mostly, though, I'd be in Sheffield, behind the goals, watching Ron Springett at Hillsborough one week and Alan Hodgkinson at Bramall Lane the next. Neither was tall for a goalie, but they were both good enough to play for England."

Young Wilson learned fast and proved adept enough at his own game to be called up for the England Schoolboy team.

"My dad refused to watch me play for them against Scotland!"

His skill attracted the attention of Manchester United and in 1957 both Bob Wilson and his international team mate, one Norbert Stiles, were invited to Old Trafford.

"I was besotted with the great United side, so cruelly to be depleted at Munich. It was a true thrill to play in the United junior team alongside Nobby - but dad didn't want me to sign for them. He was adamant that I should get some qualifications before committing myself to a profession which (at the time) had a maximum wage of £20 per week and no guarantees.

"I returned to school to get my 'A' levels, before going to Loughborough Colleges. That is where I came into contact with one Stanley Cullis!

"We had a fine football side, which reached the quarter final of the F.A. Amateur Cup in 1960. We beat the great Bishop Auckland and Corinthian Casuals, only to lose to Hitchin in the quarter finals."

In fact Bob was carried off in the first ten minutes of that game having broken three ribs. It wasn't the first time - and certainly wouldn't be the last - that Wilson suffered agonising injury in the pursuit of his trade: the hallmark of his own particular goalkeeping product was unflinching bravery.

The success of Loughborough Colleges ensured that attention was ever focussed on their tall fair keeper, and he was selected as reserve to Mike Pinner in the England Amateur side. He had attracted, too, the professionals.

"We played a number of clubs' reserve sides. One match was at Molineux against the Wolves and, although we lost 2-5, I had one of those good days. Stan Cullis made contact with me through Joe Gardiner. Yes! I said, I'd be delighted to turn out for Wolves when I'm not playing for Loughborough.

"I totally believed in Stan Cullis. He had such passion, with that animated face. I'd come along to his office where he seemed to love to talk education with me, to talk about his son (now a clergyman, of course) who was studying at Repton.

"It was marvellous experience, rubbing shoulders with greats like Malcolm Finlayson and Ron Flowers. During the pre-season I'd go up for training and spent a lot of time with Fred Davies, who I really liked as a guy. We'd train at Castlecroft - what brilliant facilities they provided. I stayed at Bill Shorthouse's mother-in-law's 20 yards from Molineux, rooming with a young man called Peter Knowles.

"During the season I'd play with the Reserves in the Central League or the 'A' team in the Midland Intermediate League. I had no money of course! Sure, they paid travelling expenses but, being a student, I'd try to get there for nothing, often hitching. On two occasions I travelled on the Saturday morning perched on the back of a mate's motorbike! On arrival I'd have a light bit of chicken in a Chinese restaurant for early lunch and then report for the game."

Wolves had a host of fine goalkeepers jockeying for position at the time. Finlayson was in pole position, but Davies was moving through the ranks and youngsters such as Jimmy Barron and Bob Knight were showing promise in the junior sides. Mr. Cullis plainly admired the ex-grammar school boy, however.

"During my last year at College, Wolves decided that I had enough potential and wanted to secure me on something more permanent than the amateur forms which is all I'd ever signed for them. They offered me part-time terms at £30 per week, which would have enabled me to carry on with another job as a teacher. I was in my probationary year, though, and needed to be very careful about where I taught. My fiancee was teaching drama, and only the London area had that on the curriculum at the time.

"The only interview I ever had was for a post at the Rutherford School in Paddington, teaching P.E. and history. I got the job, having put to one side all thought of Wolves' offer.

"As I was going to be based in London I got in touch with Bertie Mee who had been an official with the England Grammar School team that I'd played for. Thus I signed for Arsenal.

"All hell was let loose at Molineux. Wolves were claiming that their offer of part-time terms legally bound me to the club. But I'm a teacher! I pleaded, to no avail. I truly had been an amateur. I was called before the Board. Stan was there. 'Come on, lad, speak up' he said. But the directors were determined, threatening a legal battle. Old Mr Baker, the chairman, was fantastic to me, but was attacked from the other side of the table. It was an amazing experience for a young student. The League Secretary Alan Hardaker took Wolves' side. All the pleasantries of having played for such a famous club had gone out of the window. Dad threatened legal action. But Arsenal, being Arsenal, cut it all short. They chose to pay a transfer fee of £6,500, which is the first and last time a fee was ever paid for an amateur. It was the Summer of 1963, just as I played my first game for The Gunners. Jack McClelland had flu and I replaced him for a friendly in Hamburg against the likes of Uwe Seeler. We drew 2-2 and I had a good game."

McClelland started the season but, when he got injured and the somewhat portly Ian McKechnie struck bad form, Wilson, still an amateur, was summoned to the fray. Nottingham Forest provided the oppostiion at Highbury and the home side triumphed by 4 goals to 2.

"I had a run of six First Division games and a Fairs Cup tie, of which we won all bar one - at Stamford Bridge. Billy Wright, our manager, then bought Jim Furnell from Liverpool and I was in the wilderness for a season and a half. But Jim suffered from inconsistency and Billy brought me back on the Boxing Day for a game with Sheffield Wednesday. Then on New Years Day at Fulham I dislocated my elbow after five minutes and we lost 0-1. After that I didn't get back until towards the end of season 1967-68. Arsenal had lost to Leeds in the League Cup final and Jim Furnell made a terrible error the following week in the closing stages of a cup-tie against Birminhgham. I came into the side and was never ousted till the day I retired."

Retirement came at the end of 1973-74, by which time Bob Wilson had played 537 games at all levels for Arsenal, more than 200 of them in the reserve side, and most of them as a professional after signing pro forms in March, 1964.

"From a professional point of view the high spot naturally was the League Championship. But for glamour, winning the F.A. Cup final. But it was, of course, incredible to play for Scotland. It had been quite clear that I wasn't going to get into the England side, having to challenge the likes of Banksy, young Shilts, Gordon West, Bill Glazier, John Jackson, Peter Bonetti and so on. But then the Summer after they changed the qualification rule I had the greatest thrill. I was on holiday in Ibiza with Megs my wife when a Scot came up to me and said 'Laddie, you're one of us again!' Tommy Docherty had made me the first person to qualify under the new regulation. Dad was so proud, even though he couldn't make it to Hampden for the match. He died two months later."

Wilson earned two caps, both in 1972, missing out on more partly as a result of the serious knee injury suffered in the 1972 F.A. Cup semi-final but also because of the appointment of Willie Ormond as the Scottish team manager.

"Willie just wasn't interested in me - he never bothered to see me play. I'd had a rough ride from the Scottish newspapers, but Tommy Docherty had really boosted me in the press, claiming that I was as good as Gordon Banks. It was over the top, of course, but marvellous for a player to hear. Ormond didn't seem to share Tommy's enthusiasm."

To many, Bob Wilson's decision to retire two years later was a shock.

"I knew I was going to the BBC. My knee hadn't healed - today it's totally arthritic. Whispers had started about Arsenal wanting Phil Parkes and Ray Clemence. I'd achieved so much more than I'd ever expected. I deeply adored Arsenal Football Club and I truly didn't want to play for anybody else. And I'd done quite a lot of part-time work for the BBC, with an unwritten agreement that there might be something more permanent for me. I didn't want to be remembered as a has-been so, even though I sacrificed the chance of a testimonial due the following season, I took the plunge, knowing there'd only be one chance.

"So I 'gatecrashed' the system to present Football Preview, which of course became Football Focus. And at first I did it very badly! I'm well aware of that. I was truly appalling, so I must applaud the BBC for standing by me. I survived - and now it's sixteen years. Sure, nothing can ever compensate for playing. Nothing you do in the rest of your life can ever come close to that feeling of camaraderie and personal achievement when you're part of a team. I loved the daily training - every facet of playing the game.

"But I'm lucky. The adrenalin still pumps. Fronting Grandstand for five and a half hours with no script makes sure of that!"

Bob regrets the passing of Football Focus:

"It was a smashing little programme: all week I worked, ate, breathed, slept it. We put football first. No disrespect to Saint and Greavesie - but there it's a case of personalities first."

Apart from his hectic schedule for the 'Beeb', which includes of course sporting coverage for Breakfast Television, he is the proud chairman of the Arsenal Supporters and goalkeeper coach at Highbury and for Queen's Park Rangers. He also runs a residential goalkeeping school supported by the likes of John Lukic, David Seaman, Erik Thorstvedt and Pat Jennings.

Bob Wilson has a busy schedule. Unhesitatingly he took an hour out of it to reminisce with me. That unassuming down-to-earth guy you see on the telly lives up to his image.

THE COACH

"Why does McEnroe need a coach? Why does Faldo need a coach? Everyone, no matter how talented they are, can improve some aspect of their game. I watch Neville play, I watch him training. We analyse things, we pick up various points that might be done differently. There are all sorts of little ways in which even the best can improve."

Such was Jim Barron's response to my question of why the generally-accepted best goalkeeper in the world should need a specialist coach. It is all too clear that Neville Southall values greatly the help which he has received since 1987 from the former Wolves keeper.

"Once a week I go up to train all the keepers at Goodison (thus Mike Stowell came under scrutiny, too). Eric Nixon comes over from Tranmere and Vince O'Keefe from Wrexham. I've also been taking the Oldham lads."

We were talking a day after the latter club's magnificent F.A. Cup semi-final first showing againt Manchester United. Jon Hallworth wasn't aware of it at the time, but he was in for a roasting from his mentor after conceding a sloppy one: 'he wants his arse kicking for that second goal'. Clearly Barron expects the best from his charges. The successful way in which he goes about his peripatetic functions has brought in more pleas for help than he can possibly cope with, particularly in view of the fact that until October 1990 principally he was manager of Cheltenham, from the Alliance Premier League. To this role, too, he brought a lifetime's footballing experience, which is very much in his genes.

Jim Barron was born on the 19th October, 1943 at Tantobie in County Durham. Dad was also Jim, some 4 inches shorter than his son, but a splendid goalkeeper himself, serving Blackburn and Darlington. Young Jim was always a custodian, featuring for Newcastle West End Boys Club and Newcastle Boys.

"I'm still a Newcastle United fan!"

Whilst cheering the Magpies and his hero Ronnie Simpson on, Jim kept a weather eye out for visiting goalkeepers, of which Bert Williams and Jack Kelsey were especial favourites. Barron's own promising performances, meanwhile, were attracting attention.

"Sheffield United and Newcastle, themselves, were showing interest, but really I wanted to get away from home to do my own thing."

Wolves' redoubtable Chief Scout George Noakes arrived on the scene and invited the youngster to Wolverhampton during the Summer holiday along with fellow Geordie, Paddy Rickerby.

"When the season started I would travel down from Newcastle on a Friday, play for the Juniors and return home on the Saturday evening or Sunday morning. About six weeks into the season I went to see Stan Cullis and asked 'what's happening? Sheffield United want me'. So I came down properly, lodged with Mrs Clamp and signed pro in November 1961."

The Wolves youngsters featuring Barron and Rickerby proved a formidable side and they waltzed to the 1962 final of the F.A. Youth Cup. Sheffield United, frustrated by their failure to secure the young keeper's services, succumbed 3-0 in the Fourth Round. And it was none other than Newcastle that provided the opposition in the two-legged final. Unfortunately there was to be no fairy-tale conclusion for the two young Geordies in the gold and black, Newcastle triumphing 2-1 on aggregate. Wolves had a fine young side:

Barron; Rickerby; Bobby Thomson; Fred Goodwin; David Woodfield; Ken Knighton; Vic Povey; Alan Attwood (2nd leg: Freddie Kemp); John Galley; Peter Knowles; Laurie Calloway.

Barron picked things up quickly as he established himself in the Midland Intermediate League side, understudying Fred Davies and Malcolm Finlayson, with amateur Bob Wilson cropping up ocasionally to provide additional competition. After sparing appearances in the Central League, Barron finally made the second team spot his own in September 1963 following Finlayson's cruel injury at Liverpool. Within two months he had made his First Division debut in the home goalless draw with Everton.

"They were champions and had a fair old side, with such as Tony Kay, Alex Young and Roy Vernon.To be truthful I didn't have a lot to do."

Nonetheless 25,133 spectators went home convinced that they had witnessed the arrival of another keeper worthy of wearing the much-prized Wanderers goalkeepers jersey. The team that day read:

Barron; George Showell; Bobby Thomson; Fred Goodwin; David Woodfield; Ron Flowers; Chris Crowe; Peter Knowles; Ray Crawford; Peter Broadbent; Terry Wharton.

"I didn't get any specialist goalkeeper coaching at the time. We had to do the lot ourselves. Fred Davies was very good and helpful. Malcolm did his own thing - he'd just started his business and was on his way to a million! Nice fella, mind."

Jim Barron had the misfortune of appearing in the final game of Stanley Cullis' astounding 16-year managerial tenure at Molineux. Barron was blameless in the 4-1 reverse at Blackburn in September 1964, but within 48 hours Cullis had been shown the door. Jim, still reserve to Davies, did not see eye-to-eye with the new incumbent, 'Flying Doctor' Andy Beattie. But the 20-year-old had already attracted the attention of prospective new employers.

"During the close season Wolves went on tour to the West Indies with Chelsea. Chelsea's keeper was injured so I played for them against the Wolves in Trinidad. Chelsea won 3-2. Tommy Docherty, their boss at the time, said that if ever Wolves intended to let me go then to let him know."

Thus Barron went on to sign for The Pensioners in April 1965 after finding himself third choice again at Wolverhampton behind Davies and David Maclaren. His new job was to be understudy to Peter Bonetti.

"Those were brilliant times. Chelsea had some great young players on the brink - such as Ronnie Harris,John Hollins and Bobby Tambling. Yes, it was frustrating being number 2, but they were all such cocky so-and-so's that it gave you confidence."

After a solitary appearance, Jim moved on again, this time to Oxford in March 1966.

"Two seasons later we won the Third Division under the best captain I've ever had, Ron Atkinson. We had some good young players. I learned a lot, too, about coaching and management. Arthur Turner was a tremendous fellow but was never one for coaching. We senior players would practically pick the team and agree the tactics in the cafe across the road!"

Barron's excellence behind a side struggling in the higher grade attracted the attention of Nottingham Forest and the handsome keeper went on to be a hero for the lads and a heart-throb for the lasses after his £35,000 move to the City Ground.

"That was a lot of money to chuck around in those days. I loved Forest - it was a great place. It was an unfortunate time, though, with a good team breaking up. Terry Hennessey, Bobby McKinlay, Henry Newton and so on were not really replaced. Hence we struggled."

Barron enjoyed working for Matt Gillies and Dave Mackay and attracted recognition for his labours with selection for the F.A. tour to Australia.

Meanwhile Allan Brown moved into the hot seat and he and the goalkeeper did not get on. August 1974 saw Barron pack his bags again, Swindon-bound.

"It was alright. But we got to be struggling in the Third and I asked them if I could get into coaching. Danny Williams agreed and I was duly offered the assistant's job to Ron Atkinson at Cambridge. Then they changed their minds, which I still resent, having missed the chance of being the second-in-line at Manchester United!"

After a year in Connecticut, John Barnwell took Jim to Peterborough as player-coach, looking after the reserves and youngsters. Barnwell brought him to Wolves as part of the new infrastructure and, of course, he remained to become, in due course, assistant to Graham Hawkins.

When Barron's former Central League colleague got sacked in April 1984, he took over the reins for the remaining couple of games of the season.

"I'd have loved the job permanently. I tell you this much: if I'd got it, Wolves would never have been relegated from the Second. Tommy ruined the club, not the Bhattis."

Jim Barron stayed as sidekick to his erstwhile Chelsea gaffer until the end of October 1984. Two days after defeating Crystal Palace, Wolves dispensed with the services of both Barron and the equally highly-regarded Frank Upton.

"We'd brought along some good kids. Tommy? He sat in his office and did his after-dinner speaking. He wanted the coaching job for his son. The game's like that. Docherty took a team capable of holding its own in the division to get them hopelessly relegated. It was an utter disgrace."

For Jim Barron the trauma presaged a change in career direction.

"I became a partner in a Stourport wine bar. I simply didn't like it. To be truthful I was bitter after all the hard work we'd put in at Wolves. Frank and I took the club to a tribunal, just to get the wages we were owed, which didn't amount to a great deal."

Yearning for the game, Barron's next stop was Dhahran in eastern Saudi Arabia for an enjoyable year running one of their first division teams.

"Then it was literally direct to Iceland! God knows what temperature it was - snow was coming down sideways! My club I.A. Akranes won the Icelandic Cup and we got into Europe.

"After two years away from home, though, my wife started missing me! By now I'd started goalkeeper coaching and went into a finance business, but I didn't care for that. Then Ian Greaves invited me to become assistant to him at Mansfield. One week later I was offered the job at Cheltenham! I didn't like to let Mansfield down, but Cheltenham is closer to home and it was a chance to run my own team.

"We did quite well - but were capable of doing a lot better."

Wolves fans will recall one of Barron's Robins charges, Mark Buckland, a player harshly criticised whilst at Molineux but who is "doing a great job at right back. He's scored nearly twenty goals from there this season. O.K. he is not the best defender - but what a lovely lad."

Whilst at Wolves Jim Barron was instrumental in establishing the ex-Wolves team, playing games for charity. Barron himself played frequently. These days he has handed the reins to his old youth team colleague of nearly thirty years ago, Freddie Kemp.

Latterly, Jim was fulltime at Goodison Park, brought in by the returnee Howard Kendall. And, if anything, Southall seems to have got even better. Most recently the Atkinson - Barron partnership was resurrected at Aston Villa.

Jim crams so much into his lifestyle that it's impossible now for him to appear alongside his old mates. Rather he is hard at work influencing the players of today - and tomorrow. Looking back he recalls one man who was the biggest influence on his own career: one time Wolves coach Gerry Summers, then at the Manor Ground.

"He was the first person to show real interest, to take me aside and do goalkeeper coaching with me. Before that I'd do it all myself, against walls and the like. Gerry influenced me directly as a player - but also in my attitude as a coach."

It seems that there was a lesson well learnt.

LOFTY

Phil is one of the best keepers in the country - unbelievable positional sense, safe hands, bravery, good anticipation, ability to pull off the most dramatic saves, control of his area, a big kick, speed off the mark and the finest throw in the country. In fact, he is the ideal goalkeeper with a perfect physique.

It is thrilling to watch Phil at work taking a high and dangerous cross in those gluepot hands and sending out, almost in the same movement, a deadly accurate throw to the waiting Wagstaffe to initiate a Wolves counter attack. This is perfection at work.

You will find those works in the glossy Wolves match day magazine Molinews, dated December 13th 1969, for the visit of Chelsea. The author I knew well: he was a Wolverhampton Wanderers-crazy-17-year-old, who idolised the giant goalkeeper, himself just 22. That goalkeeper was Phil Parkes, the man who went on to play almost 400 senior games for the Wolves, a record surpassed only by Bert Williams. The writer was me.

Few of us have the good fortune to meet the heroes of our youth. It was doubly thrilling for me to meet, 21 years after I penned that letter, a hero who turned out to be as super a chap as one could ever wish to encounter.

Phil Parkes was born in West Bromwich on the 14th July, 1947. Sure enough, he was a West Brom fan as a boy and even went to The Hawthorns for trials, having played for West Bromwich and Staffordshire schoolboys.

"I only went the once, though - it was a madhouse, there were that many kids!"

From his days at Beeches Road Primary School, through Spon Lane Secondary School, Phil was always a goalkeeper, being a big lad.

"I played out once and got sent off!"

He played for an under-19's team in a Birmingham league as a 14-year-old and turned out against West Bromwich Boys.

"I think we were called Red Star. Anyway we lost 19-0 and some little guy came up to me afterwards and asked if I'd like to go to the Wolves!

"On Wednesday evenings after school I would go down to Castlecroft for training. Once I'd left school it was Tuesdays and Thursdays with the other amateurs. Joe Gardiner, Bill Shorthouse, Billy and Alf Crook and Jack Dowen would coach us. That was the difference between Wolves and Albion - West Brom had one coach and a load of kids."

After leaving school, Phil played for Wolves' fifth team in the Wolverhampton Amateur League, as well as turning out for his father's works team. Stan Cullis soon put a stop to the latter!

In 1963-64 Phil graduated to the 'B' team in the Worcestershire Combination "which was a big step really, because they were nearly all professionals in that team".

"Wolves found me a job with a steel construction firm in West Bromwich. Because I was local they wouldn't sign me as an apprentice. Working, though, stood me in good stead. I saw the other side of life -the apprentices didn't get that opportunity."

Phil's development was under the careful control of remarkable Chief Scout George Noakes and the stripling young keeper didn't see a great deal of the other main character at Molineux, manager Cullis.

"He never passed judgement. He'd come to watch us in night games at Castlecroft. I remember the first time. Ray Aggio said to me 'if he comes into the dressing room at half time and takes his hat off he'll go berserk; if he leaves it on we'll be alright'!"

Young Parkes had clearly done enough to impress the powers-that-be at Wolves and Stanley Cullis duly sent for Parkes' father. Phil remained outside the office as the door closed with Messrs Cullis and Parkes senior talking within.

"Then the door opened and out came dad, completely taken aback by Stan. 'He's mad' dad said 'he wants to sign you pro!'."

Within days Cullis had been sacked, leaving Phil in limbo. Almost immediately, however, secretary Jack Howley had organised the signing on full-time forms of both Parkes and the young man who had applied for trials from his home in Vancouver, Les Wilson. It was September 1964.

Although he was last in the pecking order of Fred Davies, Jim Barron and Bob Knight, and despite seeing Dave Maclaren arrive in midseason, Phil established himself in the Midland Intermediate League and F.A. Youth Cup sides alongside the likes of Mickey Evans, John Farrington, Gerry Taylor and Bobby Hatton. Farrington and, later, Bertie Lutton were amongst Parkes' chums. Sadly he has lost touch with them these days.

1964 also saw Lofty's bow in the Central League side, at Preston. And, ironically enough, it was the Lillywhites who were to provide the opposition for his Football League debut in November 1966. Phil had started the season last in line after Maclaren, Davies and Evan Williams. Maclaren had left, Williams was not liked by Ronnie Allen and, with Fred Davies injured, the chance Phil Parkes had dreamed of suddenly materialised.

Wolves' team that won 3-2 at Molineux in front of 22,733 people read:

Phil Parkes; Joe Wilson; Bobby Thomson; Mike Bailey; Dave Woodfield; Ron Flowers; Terry Wharton (2); Ernie Hunt; Hugh McIlmoyle (1); Dave Burnside; Dave Wagstaffe.

Davies returned the following week, but Parkes got back into the side at Fratton Park late in February, before playing out the season as first choice, Wanderers returning to Division One as runners-up to Coventry.

In the second game of Wolves' first season back in the top flight, the big goalkeeper saw red in front of over 52,000 people crammed into Molineux for the visit of the hated Baggies.

"I remember it well! We were 3-1 up. I saved a penalty and then Tony Brown hit one which came back off a post, struck me on the head and went in. And then, with just a minute to go, Bomber dived and punched the ball in. Everyone in the ground saw it - except the referee! John Kaye said something to me and I hit him - but I actually got sent off for 'foul and abusive language'. Waggy went in goal. Ronnie Allen never said a word afterwards. I don't think I ever got booked even after that - until I went to the States, that is."

Phil duly got suspended and then lost his place to Williams, but Allen undoubtedly preferred the young giant from West Bromwich and he played out the season from February.

Despite a respectable start to 1968-69, the management once again saw fit to replace Parkes. The word was that they wanted England's Gordon Banks. In fact they plumped for a skinny young man from the lower reaches of the League in Alan Boswell, who had the singular misfortune in his third game to pick out of his net six goals, after Wanderers had been routed by a Liverpool team inclusive of ex-Wolves starlet Alun Evans.

"I wasn't even playing for the Reserves that day and so watched from the sidelines" says Phil. "To be honest I felt sorry for Bossie - and for Ronnie Allen. I think Allen was a very good coach indeed. He was unlucky to get the sack. Even though we did better after that game, I think they'd already lined up Bill McGarry."

McGarry took the helm late in November. By that time, Phil Parkes quite easily might have been off the payroll.

"Not long after they signed Bossie I went to watch Newcastle play at Forest. I met up with Newcastle's manager Joe Harvey, who asked me whether Id be interested in going to St James's Park. The next day Ronnie Allen told me that someone had come in for me and that, as far as he was concerned, I could sign; of course, I knew immediately who it was. I was waiting at Wolverhampton Bowling Alley when I got the message that the deal was off. John Ireland wouldn't sell me."

Two months later, Parkes had an exceptional game against the Magpies at Molineux which went a huge way to securing a victory for his side, despite the scoreline being 5-0 in Wolves' favour. Joe Harvey's words afterwards summed the situation up:

"I was never so sorry to miss signing a player in my managerial career. Parkes is good in the air, has amazingly fast reflexes and reads the dangers brilliantly."

Phil had shifted Boswell into the Reserves after a nightmare for the ex-Shrewsbury keeper. How did the two custodians get on?

"O.K., really. He was a Black Country lad, after all. But he was a bit of a funny chap - very hard to get close to. He had this little black book and everytime someone told a joke, he'd write it down. I don't know if he ever used them! I never resented him taking my place. After all, he's just doing a job, like me. If someone says you're going from Shrewsbury to Wolves, you can't blame them for taking the opportunity, can you?"

Phil listed the names of the goalkeepers that Wolves progressively tried to replace him with. In each case he won back through and they went on their way.

"I honestly thought I was better than all of them. You just set your stall out to do a job. None of them did it convincingly, until Paul Bradshaw."

In the week after that victory over Newcastle, Bill McGarry eased himself into the manager's office at Molineux. Lofty was concerned about his future.

"We were training with Gerry Summers in West Park when it was announced. I asked Gerry what he knew about the new manager. "You'll be O.K.', he told me, 'he tried to sign you for Ipswich the other week!'"

Sure enough, Parkes continued as McGarry's first choice keeper, until January 1970 when, after a lacklustre display in the F.A. Cup at Burnley, he was dropped in favour of new signing John Oldfield. The skinny acrobat from Huddersfield Town never really convinced and, after five games at the start of the following season, Phil Parkes returned just weeks after having a ready-to-burst appendix removed on a club tour to Germany. He would not miss another first team game for three seasons, forming part of a sterling defence comprising Frank Munro and John McAlle as central defenders, flanked variously by Gerry Taylor, Bernard Shaw and Derek Parkin at full back.

Parkes played a magnificent role in a team which, over three seasons, achieved fourth and fifth places in Division One, won the first Texaco Cup in a two leg win over Hearts, went to the final of the U.E.F.A. Cup and were knocked out at the semi-final stage of both the League Cup and the F.A. Cup.

1972's U.E.F.A. Cup, in particular, proved a big frustration to the Wolves players, including Parkes.

"It was disappointing to have to play Spurs after we'd beaten the likes of Juventus and Ferencvaros on the way. It seemed like just another league game. In the home leg I got the blame when Chivers beat me from 35 yards. Folk still go on about it! But you have to live with that sort of thing. Football is all about opinions."

Wolves lost the match 2-1 and a 1-1 draw at White Hart Lane against a Tottenham side fielding an inspired Pat Jennings wasn't enough to wrest the trophy away from London. Lofty, though, remembers the tie with Juventus better.

"Bill McGarry invited John Charles to go with us to Italy as a sort of Public Relations rep. John is like a god over there. We drew 1-1 against the likes of Causio, Anastasi, Capello and Helmut Haller. Capello I recall especially -he spit in my face. But what can you do? When we came off John Charles told us half of their team wouldn't come to Wolverhampton - they wouldn't have the stomach for it. He was right: of those four only Haller appeared. We won 2-1 - a great night."

Parkes was too modest to comment on his own performance that night. In keeping with his entire contribution to that astonishing cup run, however, he played like a man inspired. One's abiding memory is of Haller striding to salute Lofty at the end, for twice in the second half the big goalie had thwarted the blond German with astonishing saves. After the second, Haller had held his head in utter despair.

"At the time we probably had one of the best sides that the club has ever had. The dressing room atmosphere was very good. Mike Bailey was a big friend - he and I played a lot of golf together. Dave Wagstaffe and Frank Munro, too, were pals, whilst Danny Hegan lived across the road. Danny was a superb player - he liked a drink, though!

"In all the time McGarry was there we only had one bad season: 1975-1976, when we got relegated and he got the sack. I got on alright with him. Yes, he was a real disciplinarian. You had to stick up for yourself. He'd walk on you if he thought he could, but if you stuck up to him he respected you for it - he wanted spirit."

McGarry certainly stuck by Lofty, although he did secure Gary Pierce in 1973 to put the big man under pressure after long enough with just young Rod Arnold in reserve. The chirpy Lancastrian, however, had to play second fiddle to Parkes in his first season. Phil was in sound form again as Wanderers swept through the League Cup and was ever-present up to and including the two leg semi-final with Norwich.

"We'd won 1-0 in the second match at Molineux on the Saturday and on the Monday Bill asked whether I wanted to play in the 5-a-side in the gym or go with the other goalkeepers to the park. I said I'd go with the kids -and did all the ligaments in my ankle. They told me right away that I'd miss the final, which was better than if I'd carried on in the hope that I was going to make it but miss out.

"I was honestly glad that Gary Pierce had such a great game. After all, I wanted the Wolves to win the trophy as much as anybody. I got a winner's tankard - it's in the loft somewhere."

For two seasons Parkes and Pierce shared the custodial duties at Molineux. Lofty didn't play a single game in the Second Division championship season of 1976-77, but returned for the following term, until Bradshaw was imported from Blackburn.

"Villa the night before was a disaster. I played the ball out to Colin Brazier who bobbled it and it spun over me into the back of the net. We lost 2-0. Next day I read that Paul Bradshaw had been signed. Naturally I went to ask Sammy Chung what was going on. Now I had a lot of time for Sammy - he is such a nice guy. He told me that he had sat outside our house at 3 o'clock in the morning having signed Paul. For half an hour he had debated whether to ring the bell and tell me what he'd done, but decided it would disturb the family.

"He told me that Tony Waiters, the former England keeper, had been on from Vancouver and that I could join them on a free because of my loyalty. I'd been to Vancouver on loan for four months already. Even so, I wasn't going to be released straightaway because Gary Pierce had an injured wrist.

"Millwall came in and Tommy Docherty asked abut me going to Derby, but, apart from my earliest games for Wolves, I'd only ever played in the First Division and we'd set our hearts on going to Canada.

"The Friday evening before we were due to fly out on the Wednesday I was just nipping out for a bit of a party with some friends, when Sammy rang. 'You may have to play tomorrow' he said. I told him that I really didn't want to, that I'd set my heart on going to Vancouver and I didn't want to risk getting injured. 'I'm asking you to play for me' is all he said. We won 2-1 at West Ham and 'Squeak' Parkin got sent off with Derek Hales. I dislocated my finger! That evening I came back in the car with Sammy because we'd booked a departing meal for the evening. He asked me if I'd play in the game with Albion on Tuesday.

No! I told him, definitely not. I knew what might happen - if I'd played and we'd won they'd have kept me in the team. My wife Maureen and son Dean (now 18) had built themselves up for going."

So went the Parkes family did - and the giant keeper could look back with immense pride on his Molineux career of 303 games in the League, 23 in the F.A. Cup, 23 in the League Cup, 16 in the U.E.F.A. Cup and 17 other senior appearances. Only Bert Williams in the history of the club has featured more often beneath the bar.

"People said that my weakness was cross-balls. I'll go along to a certain extent with that. For a big fellow, though, I guess I was as good as anyone on the ground as a shot-stopper. Again - it's all about opinions. I was a hard trainer, anyone at the Wolves would tell you that. I'd train all day on Monday and Tuesday. Wednesday was a day off and I'd play golf. Thursday, again, I'd train all day. I used to go back in the afternoons for extra practice with Sammy Chung and the apprentices."

Talk of crosses raised the subject of a successor of Lofty's at Molineux and one often criticised for a reluctance to leave his line - Mark Kendall.

"I never really had such a problem with the crowd. Mind you, he shouldn't have flashed his fingers at them - no matter how bad the provocation. I went to one game when he saved a penalty at Molineux. They'd been telling me that he was rubbish at crosses - but from what I saw he had no chance whatsoever of getting to the balls they were expecting him to come for. I bit my lip! It's best for him to move on - he's a nice lad."

Phil Parkes himself looks back on the March 1976 sixth round F.A. Cup tie at Old Trafford in which Wolves drew 1-1 in front of almost 60,000 fans as being one of his finest games for Wolves. The same venue was the scene of another sensational performance - on Boxing Day, 1969 when the game finished goalless. Particularly memorable for me was the instant when he pulled an inswinging corner from Bobby Charlton off the line one-handed and, even more so, a second half stop which I described in my notes at the time as the 'save of a lifetime':

"George Best worked his way through the defence and into a shooting position and unleashed a cracker which was bending and swerving for the top of the net. But Phil Parkes hurled himself diagonally across his goal and pushed it one handed over the top to safety. No wonder he lay prostrate for a full minute to recover!"

Football can be a cruel game: after a less exhilerating performance a week later in the cup at Turf Moor, the big man stepped aside for Oldfield. I vividly recall snapping the aerial off my radio in a tantrum as I learned of this calamitous selection en route to the game in question, which, funnily enough, was also at Burnley!

Another excellent performance I reminded Phil of was his display at Anfield in April 1969 when a scratch Wolves team were defeated by Liverpool through a single goal.

"I certainly remember that day - I was still living at West Bromwich and, not being able to drive, I was late getting to the ground to catch the coach. McGarry said he'd fine me if I didn't play well!

"Actually, I've never driven a car in my life. I had an accident on a motorbike at 14 and it put me off. I've never really felt the need.

"I can't swim either! The other Wolves lads dared me to dive in when we went to the States in the Summer of '67. Dougan said I'd float! It was 11 foot deep and I nearly drowned: they had to pull me out!"

Driving cars and messing about in pools are generally thought to be indispensable parts of life Stateside, but Phil Parkes required neither to enjoy himself immensely out there.

"I learned more about playing goal in two years at Vancouver under Tony Waiters than I had in fourteen years at Wolves. I was voted top goalie in the League three years in a row. We had a good side -Alan Ball, Kevin Hector, Trevor Whymark, Carl Valentine, Jon Sammels, Ray Lewington, Steve Kember. In 1979 we won the championship, having lost the season before in the play-offs to Portland Timbers.

"The family loved it out there. Our younger son Greg (now 12) was born in Canada. If I could have got a green card (work permit) we'd have stayed. But whenever I was due to go for my interview to get one I ended up getting transferred and, to qualify, had to start off all over again. Out there you have no say in transfers - you just go where they send you. First Vancouver sold me to Chicago for $200,000 (and you don't get a cut!). I had 72 hours to get there. Maureen said no! The manager was supposed to be a crazy German. He was, too, but we had two great years there. Then I had six months in San Jose and 18 months in Oklahoma under Colin Harvey's brother, Brian. Finally we were five months in Toronto. The manager was Bobby Houghton, the ex-Malmo and Bristol City manager, who's probably one of the best tactical coaches I've seen."

Unable to secure the precious green card, Lofty brought his family home and finished his playing days with Worcester City, Stourbridge and Redditch. For four years he has worked as a roof tiler, work he thoroughly enjoys.

For sixteen years he has loved helping the outstanding local football side Marston's Sports ("I'm registered to play if they're desperate"), but his number one sporting love these days certainly seems to be cricket - a devotion which made it extremely difficult to set up our meeting! Phil is captain of the Fordhouses Second XI.

"I've been a member there for twenty years, and joined them about the same time that I got married. Greg now plays for the third team and Dean is a regular in the second XI. My wife absolutely HATES the sport!

"Before I came to the Wolves I had the chance of a trial for Warwickshire, but it was a toss up at the time between cricket and soccer and they never asked me again."

Both the Parkes sons play football, the elder for Aero Lucas and he has also played in the West Midlands League for Willenhall and for Terry Wharton at Wednesfield Social; young Greg did attend the Wolves school of Excellence as a keeper, but now prefers to play up front where he got over fifty goals in 1989-1990.

Phil himself mostly watches semi-pro football these days, at places like Kidderminster, Stafford and Telford. You might catch him at midweek Wolves games, where he keeps a watchful eye on the stature of his successors.

"I genuinely thought Paul Bradshaw could have played for England. When he was playing for Blackburn Reserves as a kid at the other end of the pitch from me I thought he looked really useful. He was so self-confident, taking those crosses, half-volleying the ball out so accurately as he always did. Buying him for £150,000 was a compliment to me. I really wanted him to succeed - that it would take somebody so good to replace me. I've told him to his face: if he'd had Budgie's attitude he'd have played for England.

"But the best keeper for me was Pat Jennings. I rated him higher than Banksy. Pat was such a great cross-taker. Shilton I admire - and I rate Nigel Martyn, who's another good one on crosses."

Phil Parkes himself was unmistakely a fine keeper and played his soccer at a time when perhaps there was more skill per square foot than ever before or since. In his testimonial match played the week before he made that last dramatic appearance at Upton Park and departed for North America, an All Star opposition included Bobby Charlton, eager to acclaim a superb fellow professional. Years later, as the top goalkeeper in the States, Phil himself played alongside Pele, Cruyff and Neeskens in Franz Beckenbauer's testimonial game.

Lofty Parkes rubbed shoulders with the greats. For me, and for countless other Wolves fanatics, the modest 6 foot 3 inch goalkeeper was very much their equal.

On the fast track - cricketer Phil Parkes.

THE SCHEMER KEEPER

Bill McGarry was never particularly renowned for his wit. His first quote as manager of Wolverhampton Wanderers in November 1968, however, is a memorable one. Emerging from the indoor gym above the old social club in Waterloo Road, he pronounced to a reporter:

'I have a better-balanced midfield player than George Best, but I've discovered that he's a goalkeeper!'

That keeper was Evan Williams, but McGarry could be excused for his confusion, for there had been those at Molineux who were quite content to use the genial Scot away from his chosen vocation. The previous manager, indeed, surely must have cringed with embarrassment when Evan went on to leave Molineux to become the last line of one of the finest club sides British football had ever enjoyed.

Samuel Evan Williams, despite the name, was born on 15th July 1943 in Dumbarton, yards from the birthplace of another famous Wolves keeper, Malcolm Finlayson.

"My father was a Wolves supporter who hailed from Shrewsbury. He was stationed as an army seargant in Scotland during the last War and met my mother in Dumbarton. She was the British 200 metres freestyle swimming champion in 1938.

"Although father was really more interested in cricket than football, he was for ever talking about Major Buckley and he stimulated my interest in the Wolves."

Sadly, Evan was only 12 when his father died. By then the youngster was developing a keen interest in playing the game, though not as a goalkeeper.

"I never played for my school. St Partick's High, as a keeper - always outfield. I skippered a boy's club team, St Michael's, from midfield."

Years later when Williams couldn't get a game in goal for Wolves, he would fall back on these early tendencies, as he turned out on occasion for the 'A' team in a gold as opposed to a green sweater.

Evan Williams' first taste of goalkeeping came with the Scottish Junior side Vale of Leven, for whom Finlayson, too, had played years before. Williams was good enough to be capped for Junior Scotland and earned the attention of sixteen clubs. Now defunct Third Lanark won out because they offered immediate first team football in the Scottish Division One.

"For 3½ seasons I was always in their first team. I never played a reserve match for them."

Third Lanark had a struggling side, culminating in relegation in 1965 with just seven points and 99 goals conceded. Young Williams, however, was attracting plenty of attention through his ability between the sticks and was voted Third's Player of the Year in his last season with them.

"I was a part-timer - earning £26 a week to back up the £18 a week I was getting as a semi-skilled machinist. When I became full time at Molineux it was for £35 a week!"

Williams came to prominence in a match against Celtic at Parkhead in which he kept the famous green and white hoops at bay until 2 minutes into injury time. Celtic tried to sign him afterwards, with competition from Aberdeen and Birmingham. But a £10,000 bid from Wolves secured his signature in March 1966. He joined up with an old colleague from Scotland in Paddy Buckley.

"Wolves had no manager at the time and it was actually Chief Scout Joe Gardiner who signed me. The coach (later to become manager) Ronnie Allen didn't fancy me at all. He had absolutely no time for me.

"I always remember the first photocall I turned up for: there were six goalies! I thought: wae ma heavens! why do they want me?"

Dave Maclaren, Fred Davies, Phil Parkes, Bob Knight, Dave Kirk - the competition was going to be intense.

His first game in Wolves colours came at Molineux on March 19th when Blackpool's Reserves were defeated 3-0:

Williams; Stewart Ross; David Cooke; Les Wilson; Graham Hawkins; Ken Knighton (1); David Thompson; Alun Evans (1); Hughie McIlmoyle; Bob Hatton (1); Pat Buckley.

"I didn't play well. In fact I didn't play well for two seasons."

Consequently Williams found himself confined to the third team in the West Midlands League. His career reached its lowest ebb on March 4th 1967 when Parkes, Davies and Weir took number one spot in the first, second and third teams, leaving the Scot to ruminate in a 1-1 draw at Walsall Wood in the Worcestershire Combination.

"Life was terrible. I was being told when I came back to Scotland that Celtic wanted to sign me, but Wolves didn't let on. In training Allen was always having a wee dig at me. He and I just didn't get along. He had no confidence in me as a person. I thought him very big-headed. But actually I don't hold anything against him. He did me a favour without knowing it: he made me more determined to succeed."

"I got on with the other keepers fine. Lofty and I were good buddies, though we were always challenging of course. Being a Scot didn't particularly help down there. Phil Weir was quite a good goalie, but never got a chance. Wolves had too many keepers.

"I had a lot of time for Fred Davies. He helped me more than anyone. He wasn't the greatest goalkeeper, although he was underrated - but he is a great thinker. He taught me technique: how to dive, to throw the ball and much more. Fred was into the finished article side of the game. I still use his coaching ideas."

For eighteen months, Evan Williams soldiered on in the obscurity of the 'A' team, amply familiarising himself with Castlecroft and gaining more than a passing acquaintance with patches like Lower Gornal, Hednesford and Bedworth. With his emotions at an all-time low, Evans was lucky to have a coach in Ron Bradley who restored the keeper's faith in his own ability.

"To me my career was finished. But Ron told me that I was very underrated, that I should start believing in myself more. We played Kidderminster in front of 5,000 people. They were top of the league and we had a side full of kids. I had some game! It occurred to me that perhaps Ron was right."

After five Central League games at the start of 1967-68, the re-emerging custodian finally got his opportunity. October 23rd saw Arsenal, fourth in Division One, arrive at Molineux in a game put back to the Monday to accomodate international appearances from The Gunners' star-studded side. An hour before the kick-off Ronnie Allen confirmed that his 24-year-old-keeper was to make a belated debut.

"I was only in because they had nobody else!"

Hobson's Choice or not, 36,664 spectators were thrilled to witness a splendid debut for the 5 ft 10½in keeper. Many of those fans only knew him from the tiny print on the reserve team statistics in the programme. Two goals from Alun Evans and one from Derek Dougan gave Wanderers a 3-2 triumph over Messrs McLintock, Radford, Graham, McNab et al. The team was:

Williams; Gerry Taylor; Bobby Thomson; Mike Bailey; David Woodfield; John Holsgrove; Terry Wharton; Evans; Dougan; Peter Knowles; David Wagstaffe.

"I thought I did well - in fact I surprised myself!"

Evans kept his place, the Wolves supporters instantly taking to him.

"I don't think they ever criticised me. In fact when I was in the Reserves, a lot of fans wrote to the paper asking why I wasn't in the team. It was good to know that I had such following."

Notable amongst Williams' appearances was one at Anfield when almost 44,000 fans warmed to the plucky young man in the Wolves goal who brought off an astonishing series of saves to thwart the mighty Liverpool. The Kop, always appreciative of a fine keeper, roundly applauded Evan for his endeavours. Unlike Bill McGarry, Scousers are also renowned for their wit and they were quick to notice Williams' habit of dancing around his penalty area when the action was away from goal, 'The goalie wants a wee-wee!' was the chorus.

The People reported that Evan Williams had been 'nothing short of brilliant', for time and again he had kept at bay the likes of Hughes, Hunt and Thompson. He could do little about the early Reds goal when Tony Hateley clearly punched the ball into the net. But Evan was livid minutes after Wolves' equaliser from Alun Evans (soon to join Liverpool) to be denied a perfectly acceptable and very brilliant penalty save. David Burnside had harmlessly challenged the colossal Ron Yeats and a spot-lick was harshly awarded. Tommy Smith hammered the penalty, only to see Williams fling himself sideways to save. His effort was for nothing - a linesman was flagging to signal that the keeper had been standing in front of the line. Evan demonstrated his anger by hoofing the ball hard and high in the general direction of Tommy Lawrence at the other end. Alas! Willie Stevenson converted the re-take.

"I recall the Christmas games against Manchester United. In the 3-2 defeat at Molineux we should have won it. Georgie Best - what a great player! I played against Pele twice but I still maintain that George was better."

Afterwards the newspapers spoke about Wolves having discovered a 'new Bert' and of the latter-day Williams producing a back-breaking tip over that his legendary namesake would have been proud of.

Amazingly within a month Evan had played his last League game for the club. With Phil Parkes regaining senior status, Williams returned to the Central League side.

How, then, did he feel nine months later when Ronnie Allen dipped into the transfer market to purchase Alan Boswell? Evan Williams grins and raises his eyes to heaven:

"It was a shock to the system. Boswell had such strange ideas about how goalkeeping should be done. And those fancy rig-outs!"

For reasons still unclear to Evan Williams, Boswell's arrival meant that Parkes secured the Central League sweater but he himself was called in for the League Cup ties with Boswell cup-tied.

Boswell had a fearful time at Molineux and, following the 0-6 debacle with Liverpool in which Alun Evans struck a brace, Ronnie Allen was shown the door. Williams was relieved to see the arrival of someone he could relate to.

"I didn't agree with all of Bill McGarry's ideas on football - he was a fitness fanatic, for sure. But he was honest. Jock Stein was the same. It's hard to find that in a manager, and being straight is so important."

Notwithstanding that, it was clear that McGarry's favoured choice was Phil Parkes, so Williams and Boswell had to fight it out for the Reserve slot. Familiar pastures in the West Midlands League were trod once more.

After a solitary Central League game in August, 1969, suddenly a new door opened for the popular Scot.

"During the close season my closest buddie at Molineux, Francis Munro, had met up with Villa's boss Tommy Docherty under whom he'd been a kid at Chelsea. His keeper Johnny Dunn had broken a wrist and Frank mentioned me to Tommy as a possible replacement. I went on loan and played 12 Second Division games. They wanted me to sign permanently, but whilst I enjoyed the experience, I didn't have the same enthusiasm for the manager. I really am a great believer in being up-front. Jock Stein would tell you openly if he didn't like something. McGarry was the same sort of guy. They never gave anything out openly to the press. Docherty, of course, was a great one for the media. But at the end of the day the game is about players, not managers.

"Villa offered me £90 a week and a three year contract to sign for them; Celtic offered £49. I jumped at the chance to go to Celtic. It was October, 1969. Bill McGarry called me in when he got the offer: 'you can either play for my first team at Tottenham on Saturday or you can go home to Celtic'. He'd stuck by his promise to let me go back North if the right offer came in. The fee was £8,000. McGarry was totally straight. Seasons later when I was voted man of the match in a European Cup tie he sent me a telegram of congratulations. Typical. I really respect the man.

"It had been great to play for Wolves. After all, they were my dad's team. But I'd been a Celtic fan from a boy (my mother is from an Irish Catholic family). I had such great good fortune: I played for the best British team ever, except for Liverpool."

Evan Williams had the enormous task of replacing the idolised Ronnie Simpson at Celtic Park. He did it in style, with five Scottish League Championship medals, 3 Scottish Cup medals, 3 Scottish League Cup medals and an appearance nine months after leaving Molineux in the European Cup final against Feyenoord. The Dutch side triumphed 2-1 but Williams' side were not disgraced. How could they be with such a line-up of greats:

Williams; Hay; Gemmell; Murdoch; McNeill; Brogan; Johnstone; Lennox; Wallace; Auld(Connolly); Hughes.

The two-legged semi-final had been memorable, too, for the Glasgow club's defeat of unpopular Leeds. Evan was thrilled when a coachload of Wolves faithful turned up from Tettenhall and Penn to cheer him on.

"Great supporters - lovely people. I'd genuinely enjoyed living in Wolverhampton. Duggie Woodfield, Gerry Taylor, Alan Harris, Paul Walker, Bertie Lutton, Kenny Hibbitt: these were my pals. When I got married I was friendly with Waggy before Frank Munro came. I stayed in Penn - I still go down every September to stay with Mel Perry at Codsall. Last year I went into the Rose and Crown on the Penn Road and folk came over, shook my hand and reminisced. They hadn't forgotten me - that was very nice. I've never regretted my time at Wolves. I learnt a lot about life. Looking back, if I had my time over, I actually might not have left. I like the people that much."

Nobody, however, could ever deny that the high spots of Evan Williams' career were spent at Celtic Park. The legacy is with him still - even after 15 years retirement.

"You can't go anywhere without somebody knowing who you are. It's like having a big rubber stamp on your forehead: 'Williams, Celtic goalkeeper'. Wherever you go you have to talk football. I don't go to the pub these days. I love to coach a little team on Sunday evenings - that's the highlight of my week. But my brother takes charge of them on a Saturday, because there's always someone who wants to talk soccer or a Rangers fan who wants to have a go. Church on a Sunday morning - it's the same. Passions run deep."

Evan Williams hasn't been to Celtic Park for two years; he's disenchanted with the game generally. Plainly he bemoans the absence of players of the calibre of Bobby Murdoch ("the best I ever played with") and Peter Knowles. But especially he regrets the passing of the era of wingers.

"Look at the Scottish World Cup squad in Italy: no wingers. It's back to the Ramsey days. And then there WERE wingers. At Wolves we had Wharton, Buckley - Wagstaffe! What a player Waggy was! He made Dougan. He was 30 when I arrived and 29 when I left! Whyever wasn't he capped! One game against Liverpool - we drew 1-1. Waggy was unbelievable. Ramsey was in the stand and must have been blind not to see that Dave outclassed Peter Thompson, yet Thompson got selected.

"Remember the Texaco Cup in 1971? I went from Celtic to watch the game at Tynecastle. I'd warned Ian Sneddon, Hearts' right back that he'd no kick the ball, and he laughed at me. He got nowhere near Waggy. On came a supporter, kicked Waggy and, turning to Sneddon, said 'see - you should have done that!'

"Wingers! These people excited the crowd. You don't see good ones these days. At Celtic we had Bobby Lenox - Jimmy Johnstone! One game I recall, Jimmy held onto the ball for three minutes. Nobody could get it off him. You try holding a ten pence piece for three minutes and you get some idea about how much talent that guy had in his feet."

A broken scaphoid bone in his left wrist brought Evan Williams' Celtic career to a conclusion. He played on with the injury for half a season, which has left the legacy to this day of him being unable to lay the hand down flat. By now he'd bought a couple of pubs and confined his playing to occasional appearances for Clyde, Stranraer, Stirling and Arbroath to help former Celtic colleagues out of difficulties.

"The pubs were the worst thing I ever did - they tie you down so much. After eleven years I went to the States for a couple of seasons coaching at Yale and Georgian Court (New Jersey) Universities. I loved it but Anna, my wife, didn't want to leave our home.

"I loved the coaching. I got my certificates in Holland and Germany because I prefer their style of football."

Evan Williams cares deeply about the game, but is largely critical of modern tendencies.

"Pele, Best, Cruyff: great players. But so too is John Barnes. So why does everybody crucify him? It's a case of coming right at the right time."

These days Evan Williams lives happily close to the shores of Loch Lomond and is employed at the Faslane submarine base. He has four daughters - the eldest Rose (21), at college in Carlisle, was born at RAF Cosford and used to take great delight in wearing a Wolves scarf to school when the family moved back up to Scotland. Anna (20) was born the same week that Celtic played Leeds at Hampden. Claire (18) and Laura (16) complete the clan. Their uncle is John O'Hare, the former Nottingham Forest star.

Looking back on his own career, Evan Williams intriguingly lists his kick as being the strongest aspect of his game.

"I think I proved that in Europe. My place kicking always found a member of my own team. I didn't believe in diving to excess - being in the right place at the right time is much more important. Great saves are a bonus: it's the simple things that you must do well. That was how Ronnie Simpson was; how Shilton is. Peter Shilton is the best in the world, which I'm sorry to say as a Scotsman. But Paddy Bonner is in the top three. I was obviously a Banks fan. Generally, though, I'm very, very critical of keepers. The fact that Shilton has only just given up as the England keeper tells me that there's not been much competition.

"As regards keepers from the past: Bert Williams was a god in Wolverhampton, I know. But, believe it or not, I've never met him. I would love to."

Evan Williams, eyes still impish and twinkling despite the incursion of a worry line or two, still very much has a soft spot for Wolverhampton Wanderers and her traditions. There are plenty of folk still turning up at Molineux who feel the same way for him.

THE QUAKER

In researching this book I have encountered players who have an uncanny ability for recalling specific matches in intricate detail. Geoff Sidebottom and Gary Pierce stand out in this regard. By contrast, there are those whose memories seem to store only the major landmarks in their careers, which certainly does not seem to extend to an instant recall of individual games. Jeff Wealands falls decidedly into the latter camp.

You made your Central League debut against Stoke, I volunteered.

"Did I? I haven't a clue," replied Wealands, "I bow to your superior knowledge! I've never kept a record of games at any stage in my career."

Jeffery Wealands (pronounced Wee - lands, not Well - ands, I was quickly informed, correcting my misapprehension of many years!) was born on 26th August 1951 in Darlington. To this day he retains a distinctive Durham accent.

"My career as a boy was fairly non-descript. I played for Darlington Boys, but actually I was better at cricket as batsman for town and county. My claim to fame was that I was once hit in the nuts by Chris Old when playing against Middlesbrough Boys."

Jeff pursued an engineering apprenticeship and played for the works football team in the local amateur league.

"I was invited by the local Wolves scout Joe Mycock to attend a weekend trial at Castlecroft and went on to play for a season in the Wolves Juniors at Wath. I'd finish work on Friday lunchtime and travel down for games with the other lads from the North East, Mick Wright (who went on to play for Darlington) and Mick Ritchie.

"I went down to Wolverhampton to play the occasional game for the 'A' or 'B' team in 1967-68. At the end of the season, though, I asked them to make a decision as I didn't fancy travelling down for ever."

Hence Jeff signed apprentice forms during the summer of '68 and, shortly after his seventeenth birthday, became a full-time professional. He was one of several young keepers endeavouring to make their way at Molineux, alongside Rod Arnold and Geoff Crudgington, the schoolboy international.

"Did Geoff play for England?" asked Wealands "well, I didn't know that!

"I didn't really regard myself as being in competition with the likes of Rod Arnold - he was a year younger."

Patently, however, Arnold and Wealands were in competition, and jockeyed for position in the third and fourth teams, playing in the tough West Midlands League and Midland Combination respectively against older, sometimes cynical opposition, who were ever trying to steal a march over the youngsters from Molineux.

Arnold seemed often to have the upper hand over Wealands, getting the nod for the F.A. Youth Cup team, but then the North-Easterner would achieve the ascendancy, consigning apprentice Arnold to the fourth team. Jeff recalls that Ronnie Allen took a shine to him.

"He was promoting me forward all the time. It reached the stage when Phil Parkes was not playing well where he told me 'if you do the business in the next couple of games I'm considering putting you in'."

Undoubtedly Allen was in a quandry over his keepers. Lofty was not having the best of times and Evan Williams didn't seem to figure in his manager's long term plans. Rather than promote his 17-year-old, however, Allen forked out £20,000 for Alan Boswell. Wealands grins.

"Everything he told me about goalkeeping I quickly forgot."

Were the other keepers much help?

"Not really. Phil Parkes, remember, was only 21 and obviously hadn't the experience. Besides, can you blame him if he thought 'I'm not going to tell Wealands anything, he's after my place'?! I got on well with Evan Williams, but he was no real help.

"I was lucky that Dave Maclaren, the old Wolves keeper, was one of the coaches. He gave me a lot of advice and qualified it by saying 'if you don't agree with me, then form your own opinions'. He was a great help in my formative years. With due respect, other coaches who have never been a keeper don't have the right experience."

The new manager Bill McGarry continued to bring along the two novice goalies and, the following season, gave them the opportunity to taste a higher grade of soccer by moving out Williams (on loan to Villa, then permanently to Celtic) and Boswell (on loan to Bolton). Wealands moved temporarily out of the equation with a compound fracture of the collar-bone at Bedworth, but quickly returned to make his Central League debut in the 1-4 defeat by Stoke City at Molineux.

"Actually, I do remember that Stoke had a good team and that they all seemed so much bigger than me. I'd look at some of the names in their side and say Bloody hell! I am playing against so-and-so! The Central League was a good competition in those days."

Wolves fielded for the most part a promising side of young hopefuls that afternoon:

Wealands: Jim McVeigh (1); Bernard Shaw; Les Wilson; Stewart Ross; Dave Molyneux; Peter Eastoe; Mick Spelman; John Richards; Derek Clarke; Steve Daley. Sub - Jimmy Seal.

After just three second team games Wealands' Molineux career was approaching its end. McGarry had brought in John Oldfield from Huddersfield and, suddenly, Wealands seemed as far away from a senior call-up as ever.

"McGarry advised me to go to Northampton on loan to get some experience. Then again, he might just as easily have said 'bugger off out of the way'.

"In those days playing for Northampton's Reserves was like the Alamo every week. I was in digs with Phil Neal, who was fullback in front of me. I remember well lying in bed one night and Phil called across that if he didn't get into the Cobblers' first team within a year he'd buzz off and go part-time with Kettering. The rest is history!"

Unable to dislodge Kim Book, the 6ft 1in Wealands returned to his Penn digs where he stayed with Brenda and Denis Lee. What would the future hold?

In fact it was to be a free transfer in the summer of 1970.

"I was devastated. All my dreams were shattered with one sentence from Bill McGarry. As you get older you get more phlegmatic about that sort of thing - but as a 19-year-old I was heartbroken."

Wealands, nevertheless, went on the month's holiday already booked with his friends from the Wolves junior ranks, Gerry Farrell and Ian McDonald. When he came back, it was to a three month trial with his home town club under Len Richley.

"They had a lad called Tony Moor in the first team, who I thought was the best keeper in the lower divisions. But he was a part-timer, having a sports shop in Scarborough. He simply played for enjoyment's sake. Had he been more devoted, I'm certain he'd have played First Division. So I played for the reserves in the Wearside League. Luckily for me, Tony decided to retire at the end of the season."

Jeff Wealands stepped into the Fourth Division fray and was soon attracting the scouts. £12,000 took him to Second Division Hull City as replacement for Ian McKechnie. I reminded Jeff that the ex-Arsenal man once admitted to a love of oranges and was everafter bombarded with the fruit before every Boothferry Park game.

"Yep - they used to throw brickbats at me though! Seriously, it was a bit weird to have three pounds of oranges chucked at me in my first couple of games!"

Once Wealands had secured the first team sweater, other clubs sat up and took notice of the brilliant young keeper that Wolves had wasted. Indeed, Leeds had bid £20,000-plus for Wealands shortly after Darlington had accepted Hull's offer, making the Quakers somewhat peeved that they didn't stick out for more once they had realised that their young custodian was on his way.

Jeff had signed for the Tigers in March 1972 and, by the time he left in July 1979, he had featured in over 250 senior games.

"I probably stayed two years too long. I'd got married to Carol, a Hull girl, in 1976 so I signed a three year contract. With hindsight, signing that piece of paper was probably the worst thing I've done.

"Hull went through a period when, with a bit more ambition, they could have got into the First Division. We had the nucleus of a good team and, for the sake of gambling on proven goalscorers, they blew it. People got disillusioned and drifted away, players like Peter Daniel, John Hawley, Roy Greenwood. We started to go downhill. I never pursued trying to get away. Only long afterwards did I discover that folk were after me. Dave Bond from the Hull Daily Mail told me years later that, after one game against Manchester United when nothing could go wrong, Tommy Docherty had offered £120,000. Seemingly Hull stuck out for £190,000."

Despite conceding just 52 goals, Hull were relegated to the Third in 1978. After a season in the lower standard -"bloody awful!" - Wealands declared his wish to get away, reminding manager Ken Houghton that he'd be off at the season's end under freedom-of-contract in any case. Jim Smith's bid of £48,000 took Wealands to Birmingham in July 1979.

"Jim told me that Hull had rejected £90,000 the previous season!"

Birmingham quickly earned promotion to the First Division but astoundingly soon saw fit to dispense with the services of 'Bald Eagle' Smith.

"In came Ron Saunders, who still makes me cringe. For him and me it was a total clash of personalities."

'I think Mr Bull probably feels the same way' I volunteered.

"Exactly" replied Wealands "in the end it was just a war of attrition. He was trying to sell me, but I wouldn't go because I was on a good contract. He wouldn't give me a free. I had talks with Notts County, but I couldn't agree terms even though Birmingham had agreed a fee. Saunders wouldn't speak to me at all after that. Tony Coton, my reserve, came in.

"Saunders couldn't handle players who would question his methods. So he got rid of the senior pros

-Gemmill, Worthington, Dillon, Todd, me. The way he wanted to play was a disgrace.

"One Friday morning I went in for training and found that I was being bandied down to the park to train with the kids. As you can imagine, my dedication was not what it should have been. He put me into the 'A' team on the Saturday morning. Great!

"One day during the week I took the dog for a walk. When I got back, my wife told me that Ron Atkinson had been on the 'phone, saying that he wanted me at Old Trafford until the end of the season. I honestly thought it was a wind-up from the lads. But sure enough Ron 'phoned back and we agreed the deal over the phone. Let's face it, Manchester United Reserves is better than Birmingham's third team!

"I was second to Gary Bailey and, at the end of the season, I signed a two year contract. As you get older, you look at life more stoically. To be fair, it was a good contract. And if Gary was to have a bad time, who knows?"

Wealands' first team chances at Old Trafford were as stand-in for the injured Bailey. But what a start he made, saving a penalty from Watford's Luther Blissett at the Stretford End.

"To be honest I thought I did enough to stay in. Unfortunately, though, I didn't pick the team!"

So it was off to Oldham on loan as replacement for the injured Andy Goram.

"Even playing for United's Reserves at Blackburn in front of 27 people isn't exciting! At my age I needed something to get the adrenalin going."

Ten Second Division games for the Latics were just what the doctor ordered. Exciting times. The Boundary Park side were struggling and needed to win their last Division Two game at Barnsley to stay up. The Latics were deliriously happy with their 1-0 triumph - so overjoyed in fact that they forgot all about the herioc Wealands and got half way home to Oldham before realising he wasn't on board the coach!

But then it was back to Old Trafford and a promise from Ron Atkinson that Jeff could have a free if he was determined that he needed a new challenge.

"But my contract was so good that no other club could compete. I was stuck with seeing the contract out. Stephen Pears, however, was coming through and, understandably, they wanted to give him Central League experience."

Jeff Wealands' League career was at a close. That was decided not so much by the competition for places as by a degenerative back condition.

"I'd been having trouble all season. Jim McGregor got me to a specialist and X-rays showed that one or two things weren't 100% in my lower spine. The day before I was scheduled to see an orthopaedic surgeon my back went into total spasm, obliging me to sleep on the floor. The specialist saw me shambling around and advised me to retire otherwise there could be severe repercussions. That was a bit of a shock. I was 'on the sick' for six months, but the upkeep of this place (Jeff's lovely home near Wilmslow) costs! I joined an insurance company as a life inspector.

"Then Altrincham came in - would I go training? I eased my way in and have been there ever since, apart from a year at Barrow. I'm an amateur - I do it for pleasure. Honestly, I get more enjoyment now than I did as a pro: after all, the mortgage doesn't depend on it!

"I've said I'll carry on for one more season. The specialist said that this level of playing will do my back more good than harm. For osteoarthritis, exercises are more beneficial than harmful."

These days Jeff Wealands is a property developer, happily settled in the North West with Carol, their boys Shaun and Stuart and an apparently senile Red Setter! The sharp, bright face and fair hair, making him not dissimilar to Rod Stewart, are still surprisingly little altered from those which personified the young keeper that tried - and failed - to make his Molineux mark. Here, definitely, was one that got away.

BEEFY

Nineteen years had elapsed since I first watched Kevin Charlton in action. Yet here he was, four days short of his 36th birthday, facing up to Welling United at Telford's Bucks Head ground, showing many of the same characteristics which endeared him as a youngster to the Wolverhampton diehards that enjoy their action at all levels. The high-stepping run onto the field, last man out, windmilling his arms in order to loosen up. The acrobatic dives during warm-up and in the game itself to spectacularly take the ball. And still he was leaving his goalkicks to defenders!

Here was a man in love with his job. And here was a player of immense popularity, both with the familiar faces from Telford ranging behind his goal and with visiting fans who knew they could enjoy some good-spirited two-way banter with the Shropshire club's custodian.

Charlton's performance against Welling was immaculate, with his powerful voice booming across the stadium, demanding the ball for which he came with authority and determination. Instantly he unleashed bullet-like throws to furnish his colleagues. On the rare occasions that the Kent side stole through the defence of Paul Dyson and ex-Wanderer Chris Brindley, Charlton delighted in the acrobatic to thwart them.

At Bucks Head Charlton achieved almost god-like status. He was understandably well-loved before he finally departed the Telford fold late in 1990. To many it remains a wonder that he didn't hit still greater heights in his chosen profession.

Earlier in the Summer, over a patient pint of lager and a solitary cigar in the Anglesey Arms, we went back over his career.

Kevin Charlton was born in Dorden, near Tamworth, on 12th September 1954.

"I was captain of the Polesworth High School team so got to play where I wanted! Although I was basically the keeper, if we were struggling I'd move out of goal. I've always been a closet striker - most goalies are!"

Charlton's decision, though, to concentrate on goalkeeping might seem strange in view of his lack of inches - he stands 5ft 9in.

"Yes, it can be difficult being short. In the early years it wasn't a problem - they always reckoned I had springs in my heels. But the main difficulty was others' wariness about my shortness. Only last year John Sillett said to me at my testimonial that when he came to watch me years ago playing at Bournemouth, he thought me a podgy little chap! If that's what he thought, how many others were of the same mind? If I'd had an extra couple of inches, well, who knows - perhaps I'd have been a first division keeper?

"I was all sport at school and played for Warwickshire Boys. When I left at 15 it was go as an apprentice miner at Birch Coppice. That lasted two months. I was playing local football when Joe Gardiner spotted me. I'd been to Leicester, Coventry and West Bromwich for trials but decided to join Wolves with my old schoolmate Peter Eastoe. They offered me an apprenticeship in 1970.

"Two weeks later Leicester knocked on the door. Gordon Banks was there and Peter Shilton was just coming through. You look back and think: did I make a mistake? But you make your own bed and must lie in it.

"I was really happy as an apprentice at Molineux, cleaning floors and baths, sweeping terraces, the lot. Apart from Peter, the likes of Steve Daley, Alan Sunderland and Barry Powell were apprentices, too."

Charlton had a very early baptism into the higher echelons of Molineux. With Phil Parkes still recovering from his German appendectomy and Rod Arnold also injured, Kevin found himself second keeper to John Oldfield. He was pitched straight into the Central League side.

"I was 16 and still young and gobby. You realise what it's like at that age - you know it all, you're the bees-knees. I didn't appreciate the magnitude of it all. No, I didn't find it difficult in the Central League. Things were happening more quickly and shots were harder - but goalkeeping is goalkeeping."

How much help did the young apprentice get?

"About the same as the outfield players. The facilities were great and we were well-coached by Gordon Eddlestone and then Norman Bodell. We'd go up to West Park for shooting practice and so on, but there was no technical goalkeeping stuff as such. It was crossing, reflexes, stamina - they'd batter you. The philosophy was one of practice makes perfect rather than perfecting practice."

At the helm, of course, was Bill McGarry.

"We apprentices didn't see much of him, there was very much a wall. But we were totally in awe of him.

"I was in digs with Barry Powell. Nigel Williams and Eddie Gould were friends, too. They were great days - it was so exciting to be part of such a famous First Division club. We'd have free entry everywhere, everyone was keen for you to do well.

"They called me 'Beefy'. Wayne Nicholls was 'Zoomy' after a cartoon character! There was Mickey Kent, a legend in his own lunchtime!....."

The youngsters played hard off and on the park and were good enough to reach the semi-finals of the F.A. Youth Cup. Of the side defeated by Arsenal over two legs, only three made the Molineux senior side. The team read:

Charlton; Richard Dams; Alan Stephens; Doug Devlin; John Robinson; John Rutter; Eddie Gould; Alan Sunderland; Peter Eastoe; Mickey Collins; Steve Daley.

Kevin Charlton signed full professional forms after two years at Molineux. His prospects of reaching the senior team, however, seemed remote, with Lofty playing better than ever. In December 1973, therefore, Charlton signed for Third Division Bournemouth at a fee of £4,000.

"Bill McGarry was off-loading. For me it was a great disappointment, but I wanted first team football. Fred Davies had just left Bournemouth and I vied for the spot with 'Queenie' Baker. It always seemed nice and sunny down there! Football was fun, except when we lost to Wycombe Wanderers in the second round of the F.A. Cup in 1974. In the replay I got kicked in the shoulder and had to come off at halftime. The manager, Trevor Hartley, said I'd bottled it. Not long after they said they were letting me go. I was devastated.

"Hereford asked me to go on loan for their trip to Holland. When we got back John Sillett offered me a contract: it was June 1975. I got £50 a week. I was there for three years, winning a Third Division championship medal in 1976. It wasn't easy at first, having displaced the local hero Tommy Hughes. Some parts of the ground were rooting for me, whereas for others everything I did was wrong.

"I had a spell on loan to help out Barnsley, without getting a game, but then I decided to go part-time."

After 52 League games for Hereford to add to his 21 for Bournemouth, Charlton signed for Stuart Mason at Bangor City, first in the Northern Premier League and then the Alliance. Kevin settled happily into his new home on Anglesey.

Eighteen months later, with Alan Walker and Dave Mather, he formed part of a £22,000 tripartite sale to Telford. His new club were just above base slot in the Alliance. By the end of the season the Lillywhites had climbed to twelfth. Manager was Gordon Banks, yet the signings were not of his doing, rather that of the chairman.

"I didn't really learn anything from Banksy. Living on Anglesey I didn't go down for training much, so didn't work with him. It was a case of turning up an hour before games.

"After a season Stan Storton came in - he'd been at Bangor. Virtually all my non-league career has been under Stan, who's now concentrating on his window-cleaning business in Ellesmere Port."

Kevin Charlton had over ten years at Bucks Head and was certainly no stranger to the A5 which links his North Walian home with Telford - 100 miles exactly by way of Betws-y-Coed! Back in the Summer of 1990 it was apparent that Kevin was getting tired of all the travelling.

"Anglesey is fabulous. We have a lot of friends up here and are really settled. I work as a rep so do a lot of driving anyway. I try to work things in the Telford direction to coincide with home games or perhaps in the area of where we have an away match. I get down for training a couple of times per month.

"Yes, the journey gets wearisome occasionally. Who knows what the future holds? I have another year's contract with Telford and then, ideally, I'd like to play nearer to my home."

Kevin played well over 500 games for Telford, where he was a model of consistency, figuring greatly in their F.A. Cup giantkilling exploits and their three Wembley visits for the Challenge Trophy. His efforts were recognised through two caps for the England semi-professional side.

His club recognized such loyalty with a 1990 testimonial against John Sillett's Coventry. More than a thousand fans turned up to salute their well-respected keeper.

Not quite all of those ten years were spent at Telford, though.

"In 1988 I'd picked up an injury and was out of the team. Scarborough's Kevin Blackwell had damaged his leg in their game at Colchester. On their journey back North, Neil Warnock (who I'd known in my stint at Oakwell) rang to ask if he could borrow me. I was well-pleased, never having played in the Fourth."

Four days later Kevin motored across the M62 to play his part in a 5-2 thrashing of Torquay. Victories over Scunthorpe and Darlington and a 2-2 draw at Portsmouth in the Littlewoods Cup were thoroughly enjoyed before he returned to base.

Charlton was back in the Midlands and the club with whom he enjoyed his greatest successes. A high spot was the Fifth Round of the F.A. Cup at Goodison Park in 1985.

"Early in my career I used to get nervous, being sick before games. But as I went on I can honestly say that I didn't get worked up. The opposition start to notice that - and it bothers them.

"At Everton I don't think I had a nerve in my body. I was so happy. Happiness gets the adrenalin going, too, you know."

Telford lost 0-3 but their keeper was his usual assured self - with a style all his own.

"I don't think I've modelled myself on anyone - no goalkeeper really can. You either have it or you don't. But you've got to admire Shilton and I used to watch Ray Clemence, being a long-distance Liverpool fan. Sadly these days nobody really stands out as being unique - except perhaps the Colombian Higuita!"

Kevin Charlton has fought against considerable odds to achieve his long career, one which he intends to pursue "for a long time yet if I can play more locally". He is, you see, a diabetic.

"I've had the condition for ten years. I found that I couldn't see beyond the halfway line. My eyes were wobbling. The doctors said that it could either beat me or I could get on with it.

"It means four injections a day. It can be difficult for games - building up sugar levels and then bringing them down afterwards. But I haven't collapsed so far, even though the sugar has got a bit low sometimes. My wife of 16 years, Valerie, has been great. So, too, is the Telford chairman's wife, who is diabetic as well.

"No, I've never swapped experiences with Gary Mabbutt. If I had the capability, though, I'd like to arrange a game for the benefit of the Diabetic Association. I'd like to get other players with the affliction involved - to prove to young people that you can live with it."

Kevin Charlton certainly doesn't seem to have let diabetes interfere with his footballing life at all - "they say that everybody gets fifteen minutes of glory, fortunately I seem to have had somebody else's share along the way."

His determination to overcome the condition and his loyalty to Telford are testimony to the man's devotion, grit and integrity. He admits to the help of several:

"The biggest influence on my career was Stan Storton, who stood by his midget over the years! Telford's chairman, too, has been like an adopted father. Telford's supporters were great.

"At Wolves Jack Dowen was a big influence, instilling pride and professionalism into us youngsters -such a strict but kindly man."

Before I ventured back over Thomas Telford's Menai suspension bridge, I asked one more question of the ever-youthful, effervescent Charlton: did he regret not having played League football for longer?

"When I came out of the League I was almost relieved. It was dog eat dog. I suppose I wasn't hard enough really. I believed in what I could do but if I wasn't good enough, so be it."

Few would doubt that Kevin Charlton certainly has been good enough. And yet, if it's possible to be too nice to hit the greatest heights, then that must have been his failing. I suspect, nonetheless, that few players enjoy or appreciate their lot quite so much as he.

THE BIRTHDAY BOY

Gary Pierce lit up yet another cigarette. Up went one leg of his tracksuit trousers to prove to me that at least one of his lower limbs is not a pretty sight, revealing as it does the ravages of a gruesome set of injuries. Nobbly knees have nothing on this - Pierce's legs are a mass of scars, pits and bumps. Like many a keeper, his future lifetime will no doubt embrace some element of infirmity as the legacy of an astonishing bravery. Happily, Gary Pierce retains the impish good humour which marked his Molineux stint and made him one of the more popular custodians the League has enjoyed since the last War.

As he walked into the White Horse pub in Ainsworth, close to his Bury birthplace, it was apparent that the years since Gary left Wolves have been good to him. He beamed through those slightly protruding upper front teeth and greeted me in his ever-fertile Lancashire burr. For two hours, as he sipped pints of lager and lime, we traced the twists and turns in the life of this great character, which began on 2nd Marach 1951.

"I went to St Paul's Junior School and the Church Central School, which changed its name to the Bury Church School. I played up front wi' bein' a big lad."

(I won't attempt to recreate verbatim Gary's pronounced Bury tones in the remainder of this chapter -take it as read that the entire conversation was as you would expect from two blokes who are Red Rose through and through!)

"I was playing up front for the Bury town team when the goalie didn't turn up and his reserve was injured, so my first game as a keeper was for Bury Boys in the Under-14's. We lost 0-8 to Liverpool at Gigg. I had one of those games - to blame for five!

To be honest, I hadn't been much use as a forward. I threw myself about a bit, owing to my size. But I started to enjoy goalkeeping so I went between the sticks for the school.

"Len Richley signed me on schoolboy forms for Rochdale when Les Green was in their first team. I got a few games for the Reserves and for the Youth Cup side. But then there were arguments - I wanted to go to Bolton. I got my way, but didn't do too well in their 'A' and 'B' teams."

Pierce represented the Lancashire Amateur Youth side and was reserve to the senior Lancashire Amateurs. Whilst playing for the amateur club Sam Kay's he broke his pelvis in a cup final.

"I'd saved a penalty and we were 2-0 up. Then I dived awkwardly and like a daft bugger I stayed on. Eventually my brother dragged me off and I was out for eight months.

"I started with my local team Bury Clarence Athletic in the Manchester League. My friend Kevin Burke suggested I go training at Mossley in the Cheshire County League. After five or six weeks, with the first team keeper having a bad time, I was thrown in at Hyde and we lost 3-5. I had a stinker! To the manager's credit he kept me in and I hit a purple patch. Mind, my home debut was against Burscough and I scored an own goal! But later on I saved a couple of penalties.

"I must have played 18 games, if that, for Mossley when we played Oldham Reserves in a cup tie. Roy Maclaren (brother to Dave) from Huddersfield was watching and negotiations started. I met Ian Greaves halfway between Huddersfield and Mossley to talk terms. The fee was £2,500 with another £2,500 if I played ten first team games."

It was February 1971. Gary gave up his job as an apprentice turner and fitter to become a full-time pro for the Terriers' Reserve side. In due course, Huddersfield could afford to release David Lawson to Everton at a then record for a keeper of £80,000. This left Pierce in competition with Terry Poole, who had serious back problems, and Ian Turner (later to win an F.A. Cup winners medal with Southampton).

Pierce played the rest of 1970-71 in the Central League side, but he couldn't be kept from his big day for long. That came in the fourth Division One game of the following season at St James's Park, Newcastle.

"It was Wednesday, August 25th. Malcolm MacDonald had scored a hattrick against Liverpool on the Saturday. And now I was to play in front of 42,000 when the most I had previously encountered was 1500 at Mossley. I was overawed at first - after all is said and done, I'd not had the normal apprenticeship of coming up through the junior sides. But we drew 0-0 and I had one of the greatest games of my life. Mind you I generally seemed to do well up there and used to get a great reception from their fans."

Pierce played just ten League games that season, one in which Town finished bottom of the table, albeit conceding just 59 goals, The following term, Huddersfield conceded three fewer goals, yet were relegated again. Pierce played in just thirteen games - he was beginning to suffer the injuries which testify so vividly to his bravery.

"In a Central League game against Aston Villa I had my kidneys kicked in. I was out for four weeks, After coming back, me and a bunch of kids played against a very strong Wolves second team and we lost 0-3, but I had a good 'un. Then against Forest reserves I did the scaphoid in my wrist. I did the same thing with the other wrist later - you just get used to it!

"When I got out of plaster, Ian Greaves called me in. 'We've had a bid for you - when do you think you'll be handling?' 'Hold on a bit' says I, 'where am I supposed to be going first?!' It was Wolverhampton, of course.

"I went down and started with a medical before I'd spoken to anyone. That took all morning and carried on for most of the afternoon - Wolves checked everything! I finally met Bill McGarry at 5.30. He told me that I would be cover for Lofty, but there to compete for his place.

"It was a new challenge. Huddersfield had been relegated twice on the trot and now here I had the chance of getting straight back into the First Divsion. It was a very easy decision - Wolves had just been to the U.E.F.A. Cup Final and to an F.A. Cup semi. They were going places."

Gary Pierce signed for Wolves in August 1973 at a fee of £45,000.

"I was sorry to leave Ian Greaves, for whom I had a lot of respect. He's a tremendous manager, above all a player's manager. He was very fair.

"I thought Bill McGarry tried to rule by fear."

Pierce's debut for Wolves, ironically, came at Newcastle on September 15th 1973.

"It was 0-0 with five minutes go to and then Nattrass let one rip that was deflected past me by Scouse (John McAlle) and Pat Howard, my old mate from Bury, ruined things totally in the last minute. 0-2 - AND it was on Match of the Day!"

Wolves' team, in front of 36,407, read:

Pierce; Gerry Taylor; Derek Parkin; Mike Bailey; Frank Munro; McAlle; Jim McCalliog; Barry Powell; John Richards; Derek Dougan; Steve Daley.

A week later, Gary's home debut came against Everton. Wolves drew 1-1, but

"Joe (Royle) outjumped me for the goal. McGarry went doolally. Typical: he would rant and rave, nothing really constructive. In that way he'd just ruin a young player's confidence.

"To be frank, though, in my first dozen games for Wolves I was diabolical."

Then came a match against Manchester United and, a week later, Gary Pierce's greatest contribution to Wolves. But more of that in a moment - Pierce was continuing to recall his earliest games for Wolves.

"I'd hit a dicky-doo patch. McGarry, though, kept me in after the Everton game, so I played at Belenenses in the U.E.F.A. Cup the following Wednesday.

"A month later we played Q.P.R. at Molineux. It was on the telly and all. A nightmare! I went down like a sack of potatoes to freekicks from Gerry Francis and Bowlesy; they just trickled in."

Perhaps the U.E.F.A. Cup was playing on the keeper's mind but, whatever, he was out and Phil Parkes was reinstated for the match in Leipzig. There was no animosity.

"I was very, very good friends with Lofty. Of course, we both wanted to be in goal, but I don't think we ever had a cross word. Brian Owen used to coach us one afternoon a week, but we'd help one another.

"My best mate though was Frank Munro, with whom I roomed. Waggy, Frank and I were the smokers!"

Phil Parkes was undisputably McGarry's preferred keeper and, having ousted Pierce, he established himself in a side holding its own in the First Division and casting Halifax, Tranmere, Exeter, Liverpool and Norwich aside in the Football League Cup. Two days after that Final place was secured, however, Parkes suffered a terrible injury which made it extremely unlikely that he'd make the Final.

Gary Pierce's opportunity had arrived. Games against Stoke, Sheffield United, Everton and Birmingham afforded him valuable first team practice but, with less than a fortnight to go to the big day, Bill McGarry was worried. Pierce was too.

"I'd been staying on my line. Give McGarry credit: he sorted it! We had a training match against the Reserves on the racecourse. Over came this cross five yards out, plonk! smack on the centre-forward's head. It hurtled towards the top left hand corner and I made this blinding save on my line as I dived up and across to tip it over. McGarry went spare. He came storming across from the touchline: 'you f***ing come for everything, do you hear!' he screamed at me.

"Sure enough, in the second half over comes another cross, just the same. Out I came - and missed it completely. The centre-forward headed it into the goal. 'That's better!' said McGarry!

"So in the next game at Old Trafford I did just what the boss ordered: I came for everything. Some I got; some I missed. But when I did miss the ball, there were half a dozen gold shirts on the line to clear it. To cap it all I saved a penalty from Alec Stepney."

Pierce and cohorts earned a hard-fought goalless draw, but still the young custodian was not certain of his place at Wembley.

"We travelled on the following Monday to St Albans. Lofty and Barry (Powell), who was also injured, stayed behind to play for the Reserves against Blackburn on the Wednesday afternoon. Meanwhile I was told that I would be getting the Birmingham Post Player of the Month Award - but only if I played in the Final! Bill called me in after training on the Thursday to tell me I was in.

"The final was on my birthday. What a present! It was a wonderful occasion - walking up the tunnel to hear all the Wolves fans singing happy birthday! Marvellous! What a game! I haven't got the full match on video, just the highlights. Early on I missed a couple of crosses, but Frank and Scouse just told me to keep coming for them. Then there was the save from Rodney Marsh and that seemed to turn it. It was going to be one of those days.

"Mike Bailey played with a broken toe. John Richards had strained stomach muscles and should never have played. At half-time 2-1 to us would have been fair. But for 25 minutes after the break it was like the Alamo!"

In fact Gary Pierce was giving one of the most sensational goalkeeping displays ever seen at Wembley.

"That last eight minutes after John had hit the second goal were the longest of my life. The linesman near the Royal Box had flagged full-time and kept shrugging his shoulders when the referee wouldn't blow, much as we encouraged him to!

"When the whistle went I just sat on the floor. I couldn't run to anyone. Tears were dribbling down t'face. I kept saying to Monty Fresco, the Daily Mirror photographer: 'wi'v wun, 'aven't wi?' It wouldn't sink in."

I pointed out that when Bill McGarry headed straight for his heroic keeper, the emotional Pierce became perhaps the only man in history to be embraced by the tough manager. What did McGarry say to him?

"'Gary' he said, 'I didn't know it was you!'

"Let's be fair. Bailey, Munro and McAlle were the best on the park. But for me it was a privilige to play against Denis Law - the greatest ever. A lot of my family supported City!"

(In fact, Gary Pierce's own favourites were Chelsea - because of their style of football - and his only previous visit to Wembley had been to cheer on The Pensioners in the 1970 final against Leeds. "Bonetti was a hero - though, really, Jennings was my idol.")

Astonishingly, less than a month after Wolves' 2-1 League Cup triumph over Manchester City, Pierce was out of the team for the re-match at Maine Road.

For the next two campaigns the friends, Parkes and Pierce, shared custodial duties. Injury or loss of form from either meant that McGarry was relieved to have an equally capable stand-by to step into the fray. Notwithstanding, Wolves were relegated in 1976, Pierce getting the nod for that historic last game which Liverpool had to win to secure the title and Wolves had to win to stand a chance of staying up. A 3-1 win for The Reds consigned Wanderers to Division Two and Bill McGarry to the dole queue.

Sammy Chung took Wolves straight back to the top stratum a season later, selecting Gary Pierce to play in every match.

"Sammy was tremendous. He was a superb coach, yet could have done with some of Bill's toughness.

"Early in the season Southampton did us six, which was the only time I conceded that many in my entire pro career. It was pouring down and I was wet through. Everything they hit went in, but I wouldn't put myself down for any of them. Later in the season Leeds beat us 1-0 in the sixth round of the Cup. That was frustrating - particularly as Eddie Gray must have got the only header in his life!"

Pierce had a fine season and enjoyed the good wishes of most of the crowd.

"The Wolves supporters were superb and treated me very fair. They'd give me sweets. Somebody gave me a teddy bear mascot, but after that Southampton match it got hanged on a roof and had knives stuck into it!"

The old wrist injury struck up again before the start of the following season, bringing Phil Parkes back into the side. At the end of September, however, Sammy Chung forked out the relatively enormous sum of £150,000 for Paul Bradshaw, putting the writing on the wall for both Parkes and Pierce.

"I never got to know Paul so well as Lofty. There were no nasty moments, though. He was a good keeper - he liked his racing, mind!"

The following season Pierce got a run of three games as replacement for the temporarily out of favour Bradshaw. They didn't go particularly well.

"At Middlesbrough Terry Cochrane went past five of the lads time and again and we lost 0-2. Then we lost 2-4 to United at Molineux. I was out again.

"Sammy got the sack and in came Barney (John Barnwell). I liked him - such a pity about the car accident. But Richie Barker would have us reserves training on the rugby pitches by Castlecroft there - using the rugby goals, too! It was a farce. I was totally disillusioned with his methods whilst the young lads were really demotivated. After one blazing row I stormed into John's office and told him I wanted out."

Hence Gary Pierce found himself transferred at a fee of £45,000 to Allan Clarke's Third Division Barnsley in September 1979.

"I took over from Peter Springett and played most of the season. Then Clarkey went to Leeds and Norman Hunter, who took over, gave Martin New his chance. Again there was no animosity - good luck to the lad. But when he got injured at Chester I returned for probably the best spell of my career. Then I lost my kneecap at Fulham."

'You had a lot of injuries!' I volunteered.

"Oh, murder!" replied Pierce, "I shouldn't have been so bloody daft!

"Gordon Davies came through on his own and I flung myself at his legs. The manager's yelling at me: 'get up you lazy bastard!!'. Somehow I managed to get back to the posts - and promptly fell into the net. It took 98 stitches! Six weeks later I was back in the first team.

"We won promotion but the following season I had just half-a-dozen reserve games after a cartilage op. The whole thing took a lot out of me. So it was a new challenge to go to Blackpool in 1983. We had a fair cup run, beating City 2-1 in the Third Round. I love City me!"

Next stop was Chorley before a brief stint back at Mossley and a season as player-manager at Accrington. More recently he was manager at Netherfield of the HFS Loans League Division One. He joined them on Boxing Day 1989 with the team cemented to the foot of the table. By the end of the season he had hauled them clear of relegation and brought home the Westmorland Cup.

Pierce leads a hectic life, for management is only really spare time labour. By day Gary is Lotteries Manager at Bolton Wanderers. He retains fond memories, however, of his time at Molineux and of behind-the-scenes personalities such as Dot Wooldridge and Mel Bird. The late John Ireland also features high in Pierce's affections.

"We called him Grandad. He was always invited to the players' Christmas dinner - nobody else was. I loved the bloke, we all did. He was such a lovely fellow who did so much for the club.

"I loved, too, having a laugh with Frank Munro. He was so skilful - nutmegs in the gym. Doog couldn't handle it - he couldn't control a medicine ball! But upstairs? Wow! Then there was Kenny Hibbitt, who sweated from the kick off. And Mike Bailey, probably the best captain I ever played under at any level, yet some supporters used to hate him.

"My strengths? Talking to the crowd - that was my concentration for you! Seriously, coming off my line, probably I was daft."

Pierce paused for a moment's thought:

"No, I tell you what it was: talking to my back four. If you get that right, it saves you an awful lot of diving around.

"But you know, the standard of goalkeeping was far higher when I was playing. Don't get me wrong - I wasn't a 'great' by any means. But these days you can count the decent ones on one hand. Shilton's fabulous - the fellow's superb. Sutton and Woodsy I rate, too."

Gary Pierce was certainly effusive, however, in praise of players currently at the other end of the Molineux pitch: Messrs Bull and Mutch.

"Mutchy will go higher, too. He's such a great player, one who keeps the opposition so busy. I played for Chorley against Southport when he was there. We were 2-1 up with just a couple of minutes to go in a Cup game. Mutchy kicked the ball out of my hands and that led to a riot! The ref was booking both of us when some bloke came dashing on to confront me. So I flicked his trilby off! There I was, whizzing round and round the ref and Mutchy, trying to get away from this nutcase! 'Bloody Hell!' I thought, 'I'm not going back to my goalline after this little lot!' I did though and, bugger me, we scored another. Muggins here flashed his fingers at the crowd. They were livid! When the whistle went I couldn't even get my gloves out of the net!"

There's never a dull moment talking to Gary Pierce and certainly never a lull in the conversation. He's as honest, earnest and plain-spoken as he is apparently content with his lot. Gary is married to Joanne and is the proud father of David (18, born Huddersfield), Chris (16, born Bury when Gary was away on tour with Wolves), Victoria (14, born Wolverhampton) and Gary (10, born Barnsley).

"A baby every transfer!" quips Pierce, perhaps the mostly genuinely exuberant keeper seen at Wolverhampton since the last War.

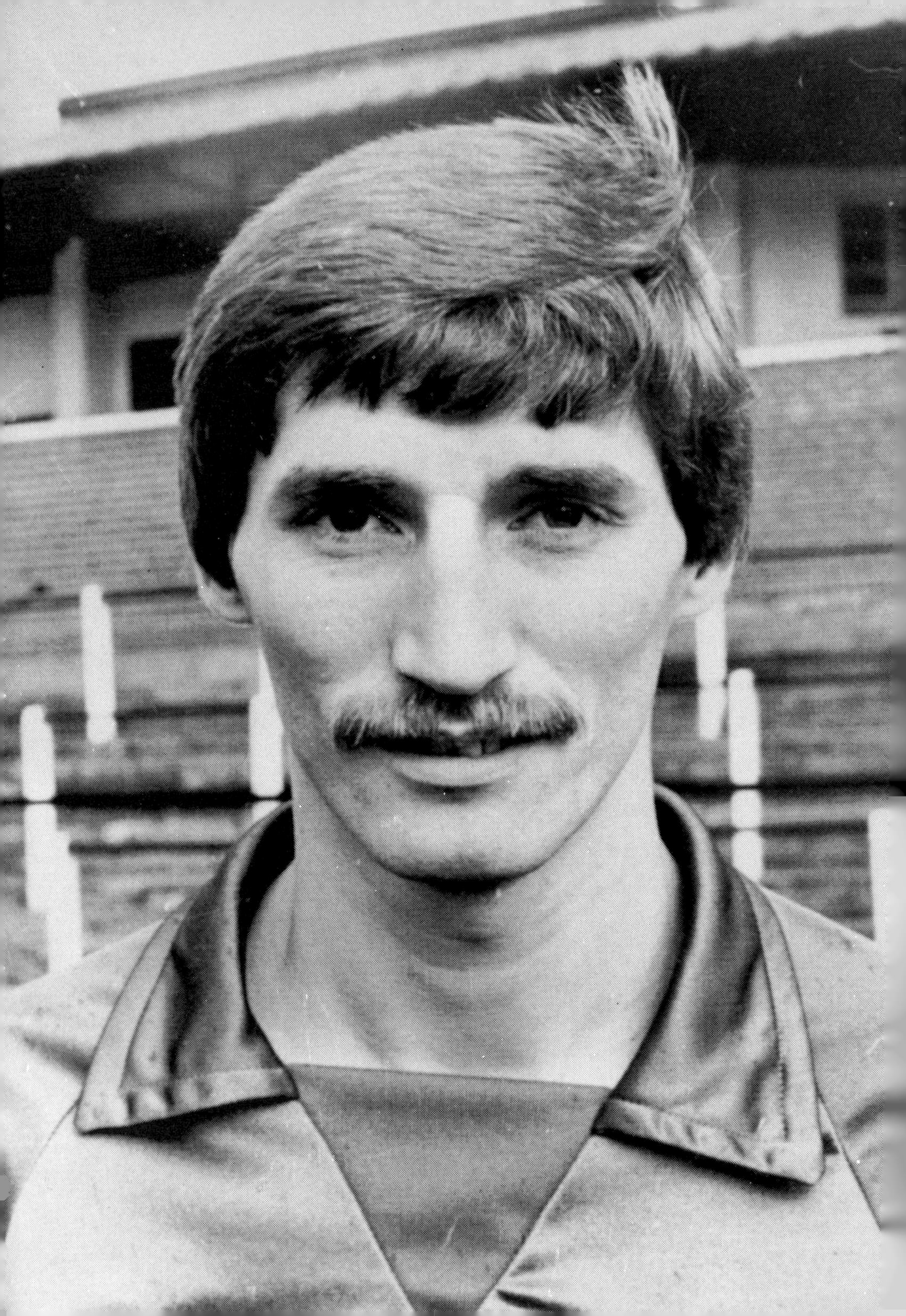

A FREE SPIRIT

Few goalkeepers of comparable Football League repute can have changed clubs for as little net cost as Chris Pearce. To date he has partaken of five full transfers and two temporary moves and not a penny has changed hands! Had a new Wolves manager not astounded many by releasing this player as a brilliantly promising youngster, then it may well have been that Chris Pearce could be looking back on a very different career, played for much bigger stakes.

Chris Pearce was born on the 7th August, 1961 at Newport in Gwent.

"I was always a goalkeeper - though I did play other sports, too. So, I represented the school at Rugby Union, baseball and cricket and I ran as a schoolboy for Wales."

Chris attended Milton Junior School and then Hartridge High School, at which stage he gained selection for the Welsh Schoolboys football team. In their Under-18 side he played alongside the likes of Kevin Ratcliffe, Mark Hughes and Ian Rush. The other goalkeeper was Rhys Wilmot, who would become a perennial Arsenal reserve before replacing the evergreen ex-Wanderer Geoff Crudgington at Plymouth.

"Rhys and I roomed together. That might seem strange, but goalkeepers often do. It's 'cos we're all mad - you must have heard that!"

Pearce had a number of League clubs actively pursuing their interest in him, but he signed schoolboy forms for Cardiff City.

"Then I got the chance of a trial at Wolves. I played a couple of games for the youth side and was offered an apprenticeship by Sammy Chung. It was 1976-77. It was an honour to play for such a great club."

Young Pearce was in one of Wolves' best crops of youngsters ever. He was in digs with John Humphrey and Ian Arkwright and close to Mick Matthews (with whom he still keeps in touch), Mick Hollifield, Hughie Atkinson, Wayne Clarke and the Moss Bros, Paul and Craig.

"I stayed with Mrs Eagle in Bradmore - the best landlady ever."

Apart from the good fortune of being part of an excellent youth side and being happily established in his lodgings, Pearce also could gain the benefit of understudying three fine goalkeepers.

"Phil Parkes was tremendous, a huge help to me. Gary Pierce too - I used to babysit for him! Paul Bradshaw came later."

Chris Pearce clearly learned quickly and displayed huge talent. Despite the intense competition, he won the award for best apprentice two years in a row. Nevertheless, the presence of the senior keepers restricted his opportunities at the higher levels and he made few Central League appearances.

His first was at Goodison Park.

"George Berry told me that when Parkesy or Piercey were playing, then they'd put a hand on top of the ball to indicate that he and Bob Hazell should go wide and they'd have the ball chipped to them. I did what he suggested - and they didn't do what he said they would! Everton scored from the resulting mess and we lost 1-2! I was still 16."

Pearce never rose higher than the apprentice ranks at Molineux. The circumstances of his departure from Wolves were heartbreaking for him.

"As an apprentice I was given a holiday every 13 weeks, a long weekend off. Sammy Chung told me to go home and talk to my parents, that he was thinking of signing me pro. Whilst I was away Sammy got the sack and John Barnwell came in.

"I got back late and went straight in to Barnwell's office to apologise. But he wouldn't take me on because I'd been late. I cried my eyes out. Bob Hazell and John Richards were there when I came out of Barnwell's office, blokes whose boots I'd cleaned. They were a great help in consoling me."

From the excitement of the vibrant young scene at Wolverhampton and his appearances for the Welsh Youth side, Pearce forlornly went home to Newport.

"I'd played a couple of games for Barry Town when Howard Kendall invited me up to Blackburn for a trial. I had a game in their second team and saved a penalty and he offered me a contract."

In three seasons, the young Welshman performed many times in the Rovers Central League team and for the senior side in friendly fixtures, but the breakthrough to Blackburn's senior side was blocked by John Butcher and Jim Arnold. His early League experience came during a loan spell at Rochdale.

"I'd played against them in a pre-season friendly in 1980. The next day Peter Madden asked me if I'd go on a month's loan."

Pearce played five Fourth Division games for Dale and a season later spent a month at Barnsley as cover for Gary Pierce!

At the end of the season, though, once more Pearce found himself in the cold with a free transfer from

Ewood Park, where Bobby Saxton was now ruling the roost. Rochdale were first on the scene with a twelve month deal and in 1982-83 Pearce made 36 appearances for them.

"But then Peter Madden got sacked and the new man, Jimmy Greenhoff, released me. That sort of thing seemed to keep happening to me: new managers came in and I'd move out!"

Next stop was Port Vale in the Third Division, where Chris remained for three years, keeping Barry Siddall out of the side for a lengthy spell.

"I've done well enough at all of the clubs. But I'm a bit daft when I'm playing - a character and that. Even so, they never tell you why they're letting you go."

But, sure enough, after three seasons at Vale Park he was off again, this time to his native Principality, and Wrexham.

"I jumped at the chance to go there. We got to the Second Round of the Cup-Winners' Cup before losing to Real Zaragosa on the away goals. I missed the last four games of the season with a back injury and when the offer came through it was very poor so I was on the list again."

And thus Chris Pearce found himself back in Lancashire, with Burnley, fresh from a breath-stopping brush with automatic relegation from the League.

"And we went on in 1987-88 to miss promotion to the Third by a point and to go to Wembley for that Sherpa Van match with Wolves. That was tremendous - I couldn't have wished for a better occasion. Two such marvellous clubs - one of them the club where I started off. It was wonderful. Peter Daniel (the old Wolves wing half) kept saying 'Remember this day. Take in as much as you can, it passes that quick'. So I literally do remember everything, from leaving Burnley on the Friday morning, through the champagne reception, to going on to the pitch. Obviously it would have been nice to have won, or even just to have scored for our brilliant supporters. I'd only ever been to Wembley as a spectator before - as a Liverpool supporter!"

(Chris Pearce's old mentor, of course, namesake Gary Pierce, took part in a good-natured knockabout game between veteran Wolves and Burnley players before the main event.)

"It was one of my ambitions to play at Wembley. The other is to be a single handicap golfer. I achieved that last week (July 1990).

"Oh, and to be a First Division goalkeeper. That's being realistic, by the way. I've a lot of games under my belt. I'm sure I could do it."

Chris has not extinguished hopes of playing for his country's full side either.

"I was called up for the Under-21's when I was at Blackburn. Then Rushy hit me in the eye with a shot and I missed a trip to France! A full cap would be nice - even just to come on as sub, anything. A mate tells me he heard Neville Southall mentioning my name as a possible replacement. He nearly fell off his chair!"

Southall is evidently one of Chris Pearce's most-respected keepers. Another is Bruce Grobbelaar.

"The things he does with his penalty area! He makes up his mind so quickly and then does it. Gordon Banks I used to watch a lot, too.

"My strengths? I haven't got any! Seriously, the reflexes are very good so I'm a fair shot-stopper. I come for crosses -sometimes when I shouldn't! - but I'm pretty good at cross balls generally. And I'm a good talker, I get told to shut-up! My missus in the stand puts her fingers in her ears!"

Michelle Pearce, a native of Darwen, has certainly perambulated the countryside to watch her husband in action. Where was he happiest?

"At Rochdale. They are really friendly there, it's a nice family atmosphere. Wolves and Burnley were easily the best for supporters - Blackburn and Wrexham were the worst. At the Racecourse, the size of crowds was pitiful even when we were doing well. But the Blackburn supporters are shocking critics. It's embarrassing just to go there and sit in the stand!"

One wonders what the future has in store for the joking six-footer. Now he and Michelle have two youngsters, Ryan and Curtis, he may choose to have a more prolonged stint at Turf Moor than he has had at his previous employers. From his past experience, no doubt he'll be hoping that long-time Burnley favourite Frank Casper, the current Clarets' manager, has security of tenure also!

*

Footnote: Casper left in 1991 - and Chris Pearce duly lost his first team dominance. Jimmy Mullen gave Pearce a 'free' in 1992 and he was on his way to Frank Stapleton at Bradford City.

NATURAL BORN KEEPER

Paul Bradshaw was born in Timperley, near Manchester on 28th April 1956. Although his latter day physique belies the concept, at primary school he was a left winger.

"I scored quite a few goals. Alan Clarkson and David Brookes, who went on to become apprentices with Manchester United, were in the same team and they went with me to Wellington Boys Secondary, so we had a really good side.

"The third year team were looking for a keeper and, being a big lad, I had trials. So, as a first form kid, I was playing with much older boys. I went on to play in goal for Altrincham and Sale Boys and Cheshire Boys.

"From the age of 14 I'd been going training on a Sunday with Blackburn Rovers. After a game for Cheshire against Lancashire, Manchester United invited me to spend a fortnight with them. But Blackburn's scout Stuart Diamond had been so good to me, giving me lifts from my home and so on, that I felt I should stick with them. They offered me my future with an apprenticeship.

"I never really bothered looking for another job. My mates were busy doing just that, but all I wanted to do was play football. I left school at 15.

"Eddie Quigley was the manager at Ewood Park. I started off in the 'A' and 'B' sides in the Lancashire League. Graham Moseley was an apprentice as well, but he was about to sign pro. He only had two or three Central League games before Brian Clough signed him for Derby at £20,000. So I went straight into the reserves at 15½.

"Roger Jones was the senior man: a great keeper. He was a big help to me. He taught me a lot, as did John Barton who was just coming to the end of his career. It was a privilige to be playing in the Blackburn second team because in those days it was difficult for any young lad to get into the reserves. Yes, it was a lot of hard work - but what experience to play against stars from the likes of Liverpool and Manchester United!

"I was signed pro by Ken Furphy in July 1973. My debut came in the Third Division one Sunday during the three day week in 1974. We drew 0-0 with Tranmere at Ewood. Roger had injured his back and so the new manager Gordon Lee gave me my chance. It went great and I stayed in the side for 18 games up 'till the end of the season."

The next campaign Jones had regained fitness, and his place, as Rovers topped Division Three. Lee was snaffled to head-up the cause of Everton, Bald-Eagle Jim Smith replacing him.

"I'd been playing well in the Reserves. Jim called me in to say that he'd had a bid from Newcastle for Roger and that he was going to accept it. I was going to be in. We were struggling at the wrong end of the table. I recall coming down to play West Brom who were top of the division under Johnny Giles. I had one of the best games I ever had and we drew 2-2. 1976-77, I was in for the full season."

Bradshaw had already earned 4 England Youth caps, competing with Barry Siddall for the jersey. His impressive form for a mid-table Rovers side which conceded fewer goals at home than divisional champions Wolves, caught the eye of the England manager Don Revie - eventually!

"Jim Smith had recommended me, but when the original squad for the match with Wales at Molineux was announced my name wasn't there. Jim couldn't believe it and phoned Revie. Don had originally called up Gerry Peyton, but he chose Eire so I got in. Smith told Ron 'that's not the point: you should have picked Paul Bradshaw in the first place!'."

The match finished as a goalless draw and the immaculate display of the tall blond Blackburn keeper can't but have impressed the watching Wolverhampton Wanderers officialdom. Nine months later he had signed on the dotted line for a more prolonged Molineux sojourn.

"I was being linked with all sorts of clubs in the newspapers - Manchester United, Leeds, Ipswich. My contract was just finishing - I wasn't on much money. Jim Smith called me in and doubled my wages, but said 'I don't think you'll be here to see it!'

"I'd spoken to Tommy Docherty and I expected that I'd be going to United. But one Wednesday I was playing snooker in the town with my digs mate John Bailey, when I got called to the ground. 'Make sure you're in tonight' was the message.

"That evening I sat by the phone - nothing! Then at quarter to midnight there was a knock at the door and there stood Jim - with Sammy Chung. I packed a bag, travelled down next morning, trained and signed in the afternoon."

The fee was £150,000. Two days later, on October 1st, 1977, Paul Bradshaw made a winning debut for the club, 3-0 over Leicester at Molineux, in the following team:

Bradshaw; Geoff Palmer; Maurice Daly; Steve Daley; Colin Brazier; John McAlle; Kenny Hibbitt; Willie Carr; John Richards (3); Steve Kindon; Alan Sunderland.

"I was pleased with my game - and to get a bottle of whisky from the crate that the match sponsors gave to John Richards for his hattrick!

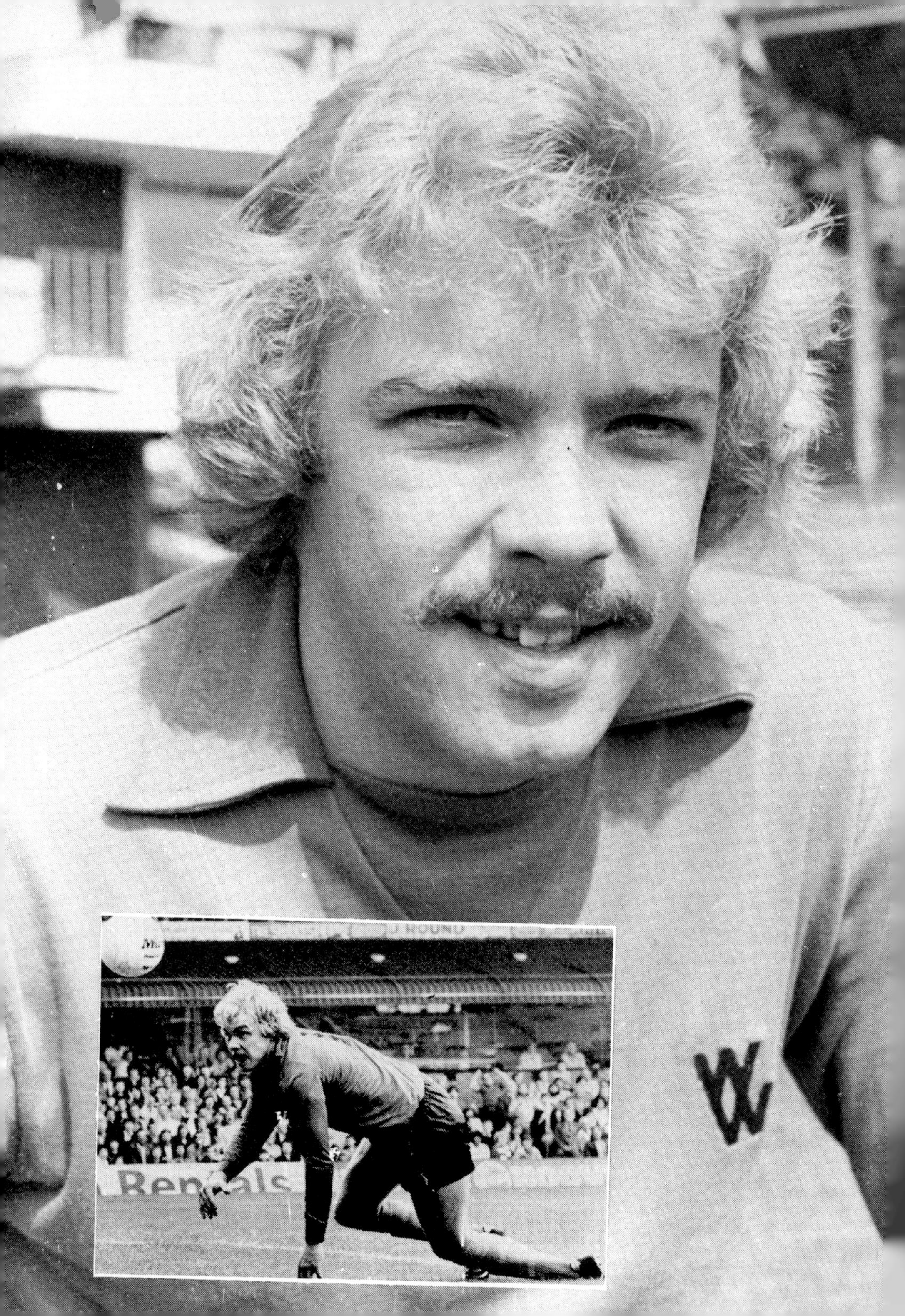

"I didn't particularly feel under pressure replacing Phil Parkes or Gary Pierce - I think they'd been after someone for a while. I couldn't believe, though, that they'd paid a club record fee for me: the main thing was not to let anybody down.

"I enjoyed it. It was the first time I'd been so far from home before, but I settled in fairly quickly. At first I was in a hotel, which I didn't like, but then it was into digs with Jack Screen, the Wolves scout who used to play for the club, who gave me a lovely home in Castlecroft. I stayed there five years - it was smashing. That's why I never bought anywhere - I was comfortable and happy."

Wolves' side at the time of Bradshaw's arrival was merely moderate. The appearance of John Barnwell, however, brought a turnaround in fortunes and in 1979-80 the club finished a creditable sixth in Division One and won the Football League Cup. This was the season after a run to the semi-final of the F.A. Cup had given due indication of future potential.

"Actually, we could have done a lot better than sixth. With Sammy we hadn't been that defensively minded. Sure, we had midfielders with flair and we were always likely to get goals. But Barnwell and Richie Barker put more emphasis on defence and the keeping of clean sheets. I used to keep a careful check of how many clean sheets I had."

In fact it was 21 in all matches, a statistic undoubtedly aided by Wolves' settled backline of Geoff Palmer, Emlyn Hughes, George Berry and Derek Parkin. Ex-England and Liverpool skipper Hughes was 'Brad's' closest friend at Molineux.

"There weren't that many single lads in the team. We had a lot in common - racing and so on. Emlyn and I bought a greyhound together. We still keep in touch - he came to my wedding."

On the subject of managers, Bradshaw's comments are illuminating:

"Sammy Chung is a great fellow, a really good coach, but is too nice a man to be a manager. He paid for that in the end. He lived and breathed football - but was never meant to be a manager. He dropped me after a game at Forest in October 1978, but to this day I don't believe it was his decision. He was a great motivator in training - things were always interesting.

"Barker and Barnwell complimented one another. John was good off the field. Richie was the tactician. He was very straight and honest, which I liked about him. Even so, Richie's tactics upset a lot of our players. Essentially it was the long ball game, but Willie Carr and Kenny Hibbitt liked to play football. Yet we were getting results, so you can't really knock it."

As we have said, the first minor triumph was the semi-final appearance with Arsenal at Villa Park in 1979.

"Losing that wasn't that bad really. We'd had a hell of a run to get away from the relegation zone in Division One and honestly it was a bonus to get so far in the F.A. Cup. It was far worse two years later against Spurs. I really believed we could win it. The replay was so disappointing - we never really played. The game just passed us by. It was always my ambition to play in an F.A. Cup final. I was absolutely cut to come so near twice.

"If extra time had gone on longer at Hillsborough in the first game we'd have won it: we were the better team for the first time in the game. To this day I can't understand the decision to stage the replay at Highbury. It was all very strange - and we'd generally done well against Spurs, too."

Bradshaw's disappointment with the 3-0 defeat inflicted by Ricky Villa and company that miserable April night must, however, have been cushioned by the memory of his visit to Wembley a year previous. Brian Clough's highly fancied Nottingham Forest side were gunning for their third successive League Cup triumph. However a spirited Wolves performance, backed up by a plucky display from their pricey keeper, brought the trophy to Molineux for the second time.

"I still watch the video. John Richards' disallowed goal stands out in my memory. If that had been allowed we'd have cruised it. As it was, it was a struggle to hold on to the 1-0 lead. Right at the end I recall a cross, which I caught. 'That's it now' I thought as I kicked it out. We played on for another two or three minutes! After that I can't remember much more. It was the emotion, you see. Who gave me my winner's tankard? I can't remember that, or the coach trip home. I do recall the reception at the Mount Hotel afterwards and the Player of the Year awards the day after, with the trophy on our table: that was nice."

Paul Bradshaw's at times superlative performances in commanding the Wolves goal earned him further England Under-21 caps. To many it remains a mystery that he never progressed to the full England side. He was certainly close.

"Don Revie groomed me for it. He used to invite me down to train with the full side. Then Ron Greenwood took over and I never seemed to get a look in. Terry Venables was looking after the Under-21's and he picked John Middleton from Forest; I was substitute. Then Joe Corrigan got recognized as an overage player and I was out. Once you're out of it it's very difficult to get back in.

"Right up until then everything had gone as a dream. If Wolves had been more successful then it might have helped me. But I never regretted coming to Molineux. I don't think my face fitted with the England people."

There are plenty of folk, seasoned keepers amongst them, who rated Bradshaw one of the finest born keepers they ever saw. They remain convinced that a major difficulty was attitudinal - that perhaps the big man was too readily distracted by other activities and lacked the full commitment to align with his undoubted natural ability. Just what he might have achieved we will never know.

Notwithstanding this, Bradshaw was twice voted Wolves player of the season. It seemed that he was destined to become a long term fixture in the Wanderers' goal. Shocking injury misfortune intervened.

"I was beginning always to need a good rub before games and the longer a match went on, the weaker my kicking got. Afterwards I would stiffen up terribly. The doctor told me that I was such a big lad that I'd be bound to have back problems."

Certainly Brad's 6ft 2½in, bulked out frame remains an intimidating obstacle.

"In the Summer of '82 the physio sent me to a specialist who worked out that one leg was longer than the other! This was supposedly causing the problem. All my shoes had to have one of the pair built up by ¼ inch. But I could still feel a pain in my back if I tried to move my legs in bed at night. Pre-season it was agony when we started ballwork. Dougan had just arrived and he sent me to a back specialist in Edgbaston who diagnosed disc trouble. I panicked: I knew it was serious.

"For two weeks I was flat on my back in traction, but afterwards was still in pain when I tried to lift my leg. They decided to do a myelogram, where they inject dye into the spine to show up problems. That was unbelievable pain - I collapsed. They found that I'd ruptured a disc and it was entangled in a nerve. They operated on the Monday and I was in hospital for another three weeks. It really frightened me. I didn't get out of bed for five days after the op. I had virtually to learn to walk again. No way, I thought, would I play again.

"Then it was back to my digs for a week's rest. I decided to walk round to the training ground at Castlecroft - less than half a mile. But I had to 'phone up half way there for a lift, being dizzy. I could go no further.

"Wolves tried to sign Pat Jennings to replace me, but he wouldn't come. So they got in John Burridge. He did well."

Paul missed the entire first team season, as Wolves stormed back to the First Division. But the astounding determination of the giant keeper saw him return for a Birmingham Senior Cup tie at Noose Lane in February 1983, which Wolves lost to Willenhall 4-3. 1,084 spectators warmly greeted the returning hero in this side:

Bradshaw; Jonathan Laws; Mick Hollifield (Gordon Miller); Ian Cartwright; Stephen Pugh; Bob Coy; David Wintersgill; Dale Rudge; John Richards; Billy Livingstone (2); Paul Butler. (1 own goal)

Several Central League games saw Bradshaw returned to match fitness; the start of the following season would see him ready to challenge Budgie for the senior sweater.

"I really worked hard that summer. I knew I'd have a fight on to get my place back, but there was no way I'd stop in the second team. The side started off badly and, after losing heavily to Queen's Park Rangers, manager Graham Hawkins called me in on the Thursday: I've got to give you a chance because you're doing so well'.

"I couldn't believe Budgie's reaction. There he was on the television, with all his trophies, saying how upset he was. Now I got on with John really well. But we were totally opposite sorts of people. I've never been a hard worker. Budgie is a fitness fanatic. I rely on natural ability. I've always prided myself on the fact that I'm not a manufactured goalkeeper. Perhaps if I'd worked harder I would have got more honours. But I prefer to do it on a Saturday afternoon, not in a training match., Nevertheless I was driven to get my place back, so I worked harder than ever before.

"There was no way we were going to do anything that season. We didn't get a win 'till the end of November, 3-1 at West Brom. I wasn't playing badly and was actually quite enjoying it, even though we were letting in a lot of goals. But Dougan, Graham and Jim Barron were under a lot of pressure. You could feel the club wasn't right. Graham is another very nice man, but he hadn't the strength required for that job. After we'd had a couple of games where we'd let in five he called me in on the Friday and said 'if you don't do it tomorrow I'll put Budgie back in'. I couldn't believe it. I don't know if it was a threat or what, but my reaction was 'if that's how you feel then I think you'd best put Budgie in now'. I knew I couldn't play in the right frame of mind under those circumstances, realising that if I made a mistake I'd be out."

Paul Bradshaw never played for Wolves again. For some while, however, he had been concerned about the tide of events.

"I didn't get on that well with Dougan and I didn't like the way the club was being run. It was demoralising to see a club with such traditions in the shape it was. Even though Dougan offered me a new contract it was time to get away. Jim Barron, who was caretaker manager by then, said I could have a free, but that it was scandalous. I spoke to Walsall, but didn't really want to go to local rivals.

"Then I spoke to Alan Hinton at Vancouver Whitecaps, who impressed me so I signed for three years. Lofty had done well - he was a legend over there! Five months after I arrived the whole U.S. league went bump. I could have stayed and played indoor but I panicked and wanted to get back to England as soon

"Then I spoke to Alan Hinton at Vancouver Whitecaps, who impressed me so I signed for three years. Lofty had done well - he was a legend over there! Five months after I arrived the whole U.S. league went bump. I could have stayed and played indoor but I panicked and wanted to get back to England as soon as possible. It was late October. Arthur Cox invited me to go to Derby for a couple of weeks to prove my fitness, but I reckoned that I didn't need to prove myself to anyone. Johnny Giles called: would I like to be number two to Tony Godden? The offer was concrete so I signed and was in the first team before long. Then Johnny got the sack, Nobby Stiles took over and, though I didn't know it, I was playing with a broken wrist. I'd cracked the scaphoid and playing on with it had done me no good. Tim Flowers had done the same one and the rugby player Nick Jeavons warned me that his had taken a long time to heal. I was in plaster for six weeks and the subsequent X-ray told them I was alright to play. But I noticed that Tim was still not being allowed to touch a ball at Wolves. Sure enough in shooting practice I broke the wrist again tipping a shot over the bar. I had a pin inserted and was out for the rest of the season.

"By now Ron Saunders had taken charge and second day there he signed Stuart Naylor. Ron was honest enough with me, even though he hadn't seen me play. He gave me a free. I talked to Coventry and Bournemouth before going back to play indoor with Alan Hinton. But the wrist wouldn't bend back at all and that was no good with the close range stuff indoors. It was the pin that was stopping the wrist bending back and it cost Vancouver $7,000 for the operation to put it right.

"Home I came and was contemplating taking proceedings against the doctors on the basis of malpractice. Then Bobby Gould 'phoned and suggested I go training at Bristol Rovers. The wrist got stronger and stronger and Bobby said that, if I could wait, they'd be selling Tim Carter. But I didn't want to risk it, so I moved to Newport. 'At least it's first team football' I thought 'people will be able to see that I am fit'.

"I moved on a one year contract with a free transfer clause at the end. It was an absolute nightmare. I was playing out of my skin, but we got hammered every week. A thigh injury kept me out for a couple of months, but when I got back there was me and a bunch of Y.T.S. lads. One highspot - coming back to Molineux with Newport. I'll never forget the reception I got: I had tears in my eyes.

"Then it was back to West Brom under Ron Atkinson when Stuart Naylor was on a week to week contract. I'd be in if Naylor left. Ron, of course, moved to Spain, though Brian Talbot was happy with both keepers and extended my contract.

Paul was very much second string keeper, however, and despite training harder than ever and being offered a new deal, he decided that he couldn't face another season in the reserves. He was awarded a free transfer in the summer of 1990, aged 34. Mark Lawrenson, recognizing the qualities of the big man, was soon in to snap up Bradshaw as replacement, ironically, for Tony Godden at Peterborough. A crucial part of the agreement was that Bradshaw be allowed to live in Wolverhampton.

"I've never left Wolverhampton since coming: I swear by the place. The people are still great to me. The Wolves supporters never forget you if they liked you."

Paul Bradshaw married a Wolverhampton girl in 1984 and they have two young boys and a baby girl. Periodically, as we spoke, the baby was crying softly upstairs. Bradshaw, bedecked in a tracksuit, sipped steadily on his mug of tea, occasionally lighting up a cigarette. In truth, he cuts a slightly morose figure, his well-groomed blond hair atop a somewhat careworn face showing the signs of a well-publicised recent altercation. He "hasn't a clue" about what he will do when his playing days are over, though admits that "it will have to be outdoors". He wouldn't mind coaching keepers, as Mick Kearns did with him at The Hawthorns and Jim Barron at London Road. Before that, though, there may well be a fair amount of playing action left.

"If I can play until I'm 36 I'll be happy. But Shilton and Budgie have proved that you can go on beyond."

Bradshaw, however, is not a fan of the 'manufactured' keeper. His idol was Pat Jennings.

"With Shilton everything has to be textbook. But Jennings would use anything. He looked so cool -nothing ruffled him. Yet he was not a great fitness fanatic. More recently I've liked Bruce Grobbelaar. What an athlete! What fantastic natural ability! But he ENJOYS the game so much. Look at most players today: they're frightened to death. Everyone is so scared of losing: winning is everything. That's such a shame."

Equally,it is a criminal shame that circumstances and injuries, amongst other factors, denied the football world the opportunity to see the true potential of one of its finest ever natural keepers: Paul Bradshaw.

*

Footnote: After a steady 1990-91, Paul was freed by the 'Posh'.

umbro
WOLVES

TO THE MANOR BORN

A few spots of rain were in the air. Former Wolves groundsman Roger Johnson pointed the way, past deserted and dilapidated brickwork and over tufts of weeds bursting through crumbling concrete. In a boxroom of an office, the graffiti of years adorning the walls, Mick Kearns rose from behind a cluttered desk to thrust an enormous open hand in my direction. A huge grin burst from beneath those beaming eyes.

He gestured to a chair, itself clearly an old friend of Walsall Football Club and I eased into it, shifting a pile of papers. A single-barred electric fire struggled in unequal combat with the grey gale outside. The weather did nothing to brighten the fading red-and-white. A hi-tec electric typewriter sat incongruously amidst the confusion.

Mick Kearns was apologetic.

"Sorry about this place! You know how it is - last venture and all that. You have to find somewhere to park yourself!"

The 6ft 3in Saddlers' Community Liaison Officer had no need to apologise for anything. For, after all, this was Fellows Park on 5th July 1990, just days before the doors would close for the last time on the lovable old stadium, scene of more than one memorable bit of giant-killing. Kearns, himself, had played a major role in that gallant past. Now he has a new role at Walsall, pursuing a hectic schedule of bringing the club smack bang into local society. Generously, this most affable of men took time out to reminisce with me over his life and goalkeeping career.

Mick Kearns was born in Banbury on 26th November 1950 to solid Irish stock.

"Both of my parents came from County Mayo in the West of Ireland. Dad's parents died when he was quite young and he was brought up in a farming family in Westpoint. Farming wasn't going so well, so he came to England and settled in Fairford. Mother came over from Ballyhaunis later. They married and settled in Banbury to bring up their family.

"I was always a goalkeeper, being bigger than everybody else! Yet I've never regarded myself as a 'born keeper'. I've coached a lot who were much more natural than myself. I played for St John's Catholic School and then the Blessed George Napier School - and was in the Under-15's as an 11-year-old. My schoolmaster, Mr McCarthy, was undoubtedly the biggest influence on my career. He put out what he regarded as being the best team no matter how old you were. Under his guidance, I played for Banbury United's under-18's as a 14-year-old and also represented the District and County sides.

"Mr McCarthy was a big Liverpool supporter. As I was probably paining him that I wanted to be a footballer, he wrote to them and I went for a week's trial. It was the era of Tommy Lawrence. They wanted me to stay, but exams dictated that I go back home.

"So I wrote to my local club Oxford United for a trial. At the time they were relatively new to the League and I had read in the paper that they were to start a team in the South East Counties League. Up I went one Sunday afternoon and was duly offered an apprenticeship.

"The manager was Arthur Turner, but the really influential chap for me was trainer Ken Fish. At the start of your career you need good professional guidance. A lot of young players miss that today. A good youth manager should be like a father figure. I was lucky, living at home, but those that are living away are not so fortunate. They get emotional problems and a lot drift out of the game for that reason. Ken Fish gave me a really good level of discipline. No way was I molly-coddled: there were times when he'd really have me in tears. But other times he'd put his arm around me and give me great encouragement.

"The senior keepers were Brian Sherratt and Jim Barron. Brian was a nice enough fellow, but very headstrong and I think he saw me as a threat. Jim was marvellous - he couldn't give me enough help. Much later, as a Wolves coach, he was still a wonderful guide.

"During my first year at Oxford I progressed very quickly, playing a number of reserve games in the Football Combination. I signed professional in July, 1968 at the end of that year."

Kearns' next season was spent consolidating his position as understudy to Barron. His big chance in the Second Division came on Good Friday, March 27th, 1969.

"Twenty minutes before kick-off against Leicester I didn't know I was playing. In fact I was in the Manor Ground stand munching on a meat pie when the tannoy blurted out 'Will Mick Kearns report to the main office'! Jim had passed himself fit, but the doctor had taken one look at his toe and said no."

So the 18-year-old Kearns stood as last line in a team featuring ex-Wanderer Brian Thompson and erstwhile Molineux apprentice Ron Atkinson to face the likes of Ally Brown, Len Glover, David Nish and ex-Wolf John Farrington. In the opposing goal was a youngster by the name of Shilton. A goal from Bobby Roberts spoiled Mick's day in front of 16,741 spectators.

The following day Mick enjoyed a goalless draw at Cardiff, who included the formidable striking partnership of Brian Clark and John Toshack, aided and abetted by another ex-Molineux star and master of the elongated throw, Bobby Woodruff.

"I hadn't much to do in my debut, but at Ninian Park I had a really good game. Then on the Tuesday we went to Villa Park and drew 0-0. I had one of those days. If I'd turned my back on the ball it would have hit me on the head and stayed out! Villa went on to get relegated and their Banbury-based fans insisted that I was the bloke who put them into the Third! But that didn't stop me being left out for the next game. I'd been in the clouds and I couldn't see why manager Gerry Summers (the ex-Wolves coach) had to bring back Jim. Looking back, of course, he did the right thing."

The young keeper, however, had done enough to reveal his promise and in June 1970 Oxford were able to realise their record fee for Barron, £35,000 from Nottingham Forest. The next season Mick Kearns was a fixture in the 'U's goal, before finding his place challenged by another local lad, Roy Burton.

"I suffered a loss of form and was keen to get away. I went to Plymouth on loan, but played just the one game against Halifax before breaking my leg in training. It was a pity - I'd have been happy to move to Home Park.

"I'd recovered by February and went for four games to Charlton. They reckoned that they'd sign me if I did well, but in reality they only wanted me until John Dunn got his form back."

In July 1973 Mick made his first permanent move - to Walsall for a reputed £15,000, signed by Ronnie Allen as replacement for Bob Wesson.

"It was a marvellous move for me. I'm not certain, but I may have been Ken Wheldon's first money signing. I had such happy times as a player here. We were unlucky one season under Dave Mackay and could have gone up, but the high spots were the cup runs.

"In 1974-75 we won through to play Manchester United at Old Trafford in the third round of the F.A. Cup. I remember getting a phone call at the hotel from the Weekly News, some local hack saying 'Do you realise that only John Jackson of Orient has not let a goal in here all season?' I told him that today he'd see another. In truth, apart from a late free-kick, I hadn't much to do. Alan Buckley had a couple of chances to win it but we drew no goals and then beat them 3-2 in the replay at Fellows Park. After beating the previous season's finalists Newcastle in the next round we went out to Birmingham in the fifth.

"Then two years later I had probably my best-ever game for Walsall. We drew one-each at Chesterfield in the Second Round (ex-Wolves Brian Caswell and Alun Evans were team mates) and then no goals at Fellows Park. The second replay was at Derby, where Chesterfield absolutely annihilated us. But once again I couldn't put a foot wrong. With ten minutes left Miah Dennehy crossed for Bernie Wright to give us a 1-0 win. We lost 1-0 to United at Old Trafford in the next round in front of nearly 49,000."

After 249 League games in six years, why did Mick feel himself ready for a change of direction in July 1979?

"We'd had a few changes of manager. Dave Mackay was the pick of the crop. When he got the chance to go to Kuwait I'm not sure they replaced him as they should've. I subscribe to the view that if you have a change following success then you should appoint from within. If, however, you change through failure then you should appoint from outside. I reckoned Walsall should have given the job to Des Anderson. Instead they went for Alan Ashman, a smashing bloke but not the right man at the time. The club lost its way. We had a couple of swift changes and my form went a bit. I was playing for Ireland and probably got a bit too big for my boots, so I went on the list.

"I talked terms with Philadelphia Furies, but didn't feel that the contract was worth the paper it was written on. You could walk into a ground one day and find you'd been transferred to the other end of the country.

"John Jarman (the Wolves youth coach) was part of the Ireland set-up and 'phoned to see if I was interested in joining Wolves to put pressure on Paul Bradshaw. John Barnwell was just recovering from his accident and Richie Barker was conducting affairs. I saw it as an opportunity to progress.

"It never worked out quite as I would have wished. I didn't play as many games as I wanted. But Paul, apart from one spell when I was aggrieved not to be in, was superb - the best player at the club."

When the call did come, Kearns had a stiff opener, replacing the injured Bradshaw in the fifth round of the F.A. Cup against Watford at Molineux in February 1980. He was 29. Wolves went down 0-3 in front of the Match of the Day cameras in a game marred by the terrible leg break suffered by John McAlle as soon as he entered the fray.

"I don't believe I was at fault with any of the goals, yet I didn't feel truly comfortable. Quite simply, I was rusty. I put that down to reserve team football. I hadn't played a game for two months, what with games called off for wet pitches, shortage of players and the like."

Wolves fielded the following side in front of 32,860 observers:

Kearns; Geoff Palmer; Derek Parkin; Peter Daniel; Emlyn Hughes; George Berry; Ken Hibbitt (John McAlle); Willie Carr; Andy Gray; John Richards; Mel Eves.

In three years at Wolverhampton Mick played just nine Division One games.

"Nevertheless, I enjoyed it. It was educational - training and working with some of the best players in the country, just as I was when with the Ireland team. But it was frustrating, too. I was working so hard to get into the first team, yet couldn't break through. All credit to Brad, though, he was outstanding.

"Season 1989-90 I coached Paul Bradshaw at the Albion. Do you know what? He is the most natural keeper I ever worked with. I told him when I was at Wolves that I expected him to make the England side. But I don't think he ever believed in himself. Before Jim Barron came back to Molineux I used to take Paul. He's like other natural goalkeepers: he doesn't seem to have the appetite for hard work. That's why Peter Shilton deserves so much recognition - there's someone who combines hard work with genuine ability."

Alan Buckley brought Kearns back to the Walsall fold.

"The game was going through a funny spell. Players weren't getting long contracts. We were settled where we were living and I didn't really want to move away for just a one or two year deal. We had a small child, so moving to Walsall suited me fine. I enjoyed my spell back here. But then, all of a sudden, I was out of the side. What to do?"

In fact he took over as steward of Aldridge Conservative Club. Goalkeeping crises 'back at base' however brought him unexpectedly into emergency action on above one occasion.

"The day I announced that I was due to retire Ron Green dislocated his shoulder. They couldn't get anyone on loan for the League Cup game with Shrewsbury because nobody wanted their keepers cup-tied. So I came back and played in all the matches up to the Liverpool semi-final."

That run in 1983-84 included the emotional tanning of Arsenal, a game which re-created the club's finest moment from the Twenties. To this day many Saddlers fans are convinced that, had Kearns not been replaced for the semi-final, their club would have made its first trip to Wembley.

The high spot of Mick Kearns' career, however, was his recognition by the Republic of Ireland.

"Particularly so for a player in the Third Division for most of his career. It was strange - there I was playing in front of two or three thousand on a Saturday and then going off to appear before a full house for my country."

Kearns debut for Eire was in 1970 as a substitute for Alan Kelly with 30 minutes to go of a game against Poland.

"I was so pumped up with adrenalin that the first time I kicked the ball it bounced once and shot over the crossbar at the other end! I don't think I could ever do that again but they took to me in Dublin after that!"

Nevertheless, it was four years before he appeared next, ironically as a substitute against Poland again. A Miah Dennehy goal secured a win for the Republic just a week after the East Europeans, Tomaszewski included, had removed Alf Ramsey's England from the World Cup.

Despite competition from Peter Thomas, Paddy Roche and Gerry Peyton, Mick Kearns won 18 caps for Eire, two of them whilst in the employ of Wolverhampton Wanderers.

These days Mick passes on his vast experience to others, taking the keepers at Walsall and West Brom.

"Looking back, I myself was lucky to have such excellent mentors as Jim Barron and Alan Kelly."

Since January 1989, Mick Kearns has been the Community Liaison Officer with Walsall. He is ideally suited to the role, being, a caring, approachable man with a heart as big as his stature - someone who feels deeply about the responsibility which a football club has to its immediate environment, but more so, since my early interview with Mick, his environment has changed - having moved to Walsall's new home at Bescot Stadium.

Author Charlie Bamforth with Mick Kearns.

BUDGIE

"I studied a series of goalkeepers. I've tried to copy Shilton's strength; Banks' calmness; Bonetti's agility; Yashin's presence. I've tried to wrap them into one. Because of having a similar build and a similar attitude to training, people said I copied Shilton. But that's rubbish. I watched each of them and have learned from them all."

John Burridge is an obsessional goalkeeper, the workaholic custodian. He is single-minded in his pursuit of excellence. Attempting to tie him down for just a few minutes was some feat, believe me. That I snatched the briefest of conversations after several months endeavour is testimony to his compulsive desire to achieve perfection in his chosen profession, with a dedication, the like of which no other goalkeeper surely can have matched.

That he is still at a pinnacle of performance at 40 years of age, over two decades after entering the Football League arena, is evidence aplenty to show that his methods and attitudes are correct.

John Burridge, 'Budgie' to all, was born on 3rd December, 1951 at Cliston, a mining village near Workington in Cumbria.

"I was brought up very hard. It was a tough drinking, smoking mining village. I was knocked about a bit. It was a world completely different to today's. Pit clogs - the smoking and drinking was all the miners had for 'escape'.

"We hadn't much money. The only thing we kids had was football. If we could get hold of an old ball then the whole village played. A lot of pro's came out of those villages: the likes of Joe Wilson (the old Wolves right-back) and Steve McCall, for instance. After homework and mi' tea every afternoon I'd be off goalkeeping - I was always a keeper. The stretch where we used to play - the 'tennis court' - is still there. And do you know what? There's nobody playing there today. As a kid you could always get a game. But now there's nobody. And that's what's wrong with the game: it's not there at grass-roots. The game's faster, oh aye, but the skill is not there. As kids, everyone could kick with both feet in our time. Nowadays there's youngsters coming into clubs who cannot even kick properly with one foot. 'Grass-cutters' - well-struck - they cannot do 'em. Oh, they can bend it with the side of their boot, but if I ask a youngster to put over a good solid cross, then they've no idea. And so there are no individuals - and that's why the game's going long ball."

John played for Workington schoolboys and for the county and went for trials for the England boys side.

"But I might as well not have bothered, the team was picked already. You don't see many schoolboy internationals making it to the top, do you? It's a case of who you are and who's pushing you.

"I had the chance of trials at Stoke City and Carlisle, but I signed apprentice for my local club, Workington. Dad had silicosis and had to come out of the pit. Mother needed the money and I was now the breadwinner. It was 1968-69 and I got £5 a week, plus bonuses - a hell of a lot in those days.

"At the time you were a hero in those villages if you worked down the mine and played for Workington Rugby League Club's 'A' team. Hard as nails, those blokes were. That's what dad wanted me to do. I was good enough, too: I played for the county at rugby as well as football. But I always wanted to be a professional footballer."

Burridge signed full professional forms for Workington in January 1970, a season after making his Fourth Division debut. In 1970-71 he replaced the senior man, Mike Rogan, 26 times in the first team and attracted the attention of Blackpool's manager Bob Stokoe.

"Four days before my 19th birthday, Brian Doyle called me into his office to tell me that he was selling me to Blackpool. I told him that I wasn't so sure about that, what with the money situation at home. He came to the house and mother told him I couldn't really go. But I did go, on the Wednesday, with my clothes wrapped in a brown paper parcel. I signed for £35 a week - Blackpool were still in the First Division then, remember. £10 per week I sent home to mother. I had £15 a week appearance money if I was in the first team and £1,000 signing-on fee paid into the bank. All my digs were paid for, too. It was a hell of a lot!

"My debut was at Everton and I had a blinding game in a 0-0 draw."

Burridge was the fifth keeper employed by the Tangerines in 1970-71, after Adam Blacklaw, Harry Thomson, Alan Taylor and Neil Ramsbottom. In just 3 appearances he couldn't prevent, of course, Blackpool's relegation. The following season, however, he was first-choice as the Seasiders consolidated in sixth place in Division Two.

For four seasons, Blackpool were there or thereabouts in the table, their eager young keeper attracting plenty of attention with some excellent performances for a team very tight on goals conceded. 1971 saw them win the Anglo-Italian Cup 2-1 over Bologna, a competition in which they were losing finalists a year later, 1-3 to A.S. Roma.

With the big Scot George Wood ready to take over at Bloomfield Road, Aston Villa were allowed to secure John's services in September 1975 for £100,000, ten times the fee for which Blackpool had obtained him. That differential, plus the 134 League games which Budgie served, meant that Blackpool had excellent value.

Budgie himself took away from the breezy Lancashire resort a local girl, Janet, who became his wife when they moved down the M6. Home duly established in Elford, Budgie set about serving his new paymasters. For two seasons he performed sterlingly at Villa Park for a team good enough to take fourth place in Division One in 1976-77 as well as win the League Cup in a twice-replayed epic over Everton. Brian Little, later to manage Wolves, scored two of the goals which finally brought home the trophy from Old Trafford for a team which also included Gordon Smith, who would be a colleague of Burridge's years later at Molineux. Another future Wanderer, Andy King, was with the disappointed losers.

"But Ron Saunders wouldn't let me train the way I wanted. He used to restrict me - let's leave it at that. I don't want to say any more."

It was time for Budgie to fly again. First stop was a temporary transfer to Roots Hall.

"I knew I was going to Crystal Palace, but they were happy for me to help out Southend. I did it as a favour to Dave Smith, who has never forgotten it. He still calls my wife his adopted daughter. I played six games and we drew one and won the rest. They got promoted."

A £65,000 cheque took John Burridge to Selhurst Park and Terry Venables.

"Terry was the best manager I ever had - by far. He knows the game inside out. Playing for him was playing without a burden. Nothing was any trouble, everything was revolutionary. He used anything to make a player better - hypnotism, food, different kinds of boots, gloves...In 1978 he was years ahead of his time. He still is. It was a pleasure to play for him. I can't express....he should have been the England manager."

Budgie arrived in South London in March 1978. The following season he was an ever-present as the Eagles took the Second Division championship, conceding a miserly 24 goals.

"I loved London, I still do. I'd go back tomorrow. It was exciting to play there - the big city."

Almost three years after arriving in 'The Smoke', Budgie moved across London. Less than three weeks after Venables, Burridge followed him to Queen's Park Rangers. The extrovert manager had seen enough of his keeper to decide that £200,000 would be money well-spent to replace Chris Woods.

"I loved it there, too. But then they installed Astroturf. I couldn't train on that one week and be expected to perform on grass the next. So I moved on.

"I wasn't going to go to Wolves, rather Coventry. Jim Gregory at Rangers, though, wanted to get his investment back. Wolves offered £100,000 and Coventry only half as much. There was only one place Jim Gregory was going to let me go."

And so John signed for Wanderers, several weeks after first arriving at Molineux on loan.

They were strange days at Molineux, the club having been 'reprieved' when it seemed that they were irretrievably headed for extinction. Derek Dougan's gang of mystery 'benefactors' ruled the roost and Graham Hawkins was installed in the managerial seat.

Just days after the 'rescue package', Wolves took to the Molineux turf with a fledgling side, boosted at the back by the vastly experienced and characterful Burridge. In an emotionally-explosive setting, Blackburn Rovers were incidental attractions as the young Wolves fought for a 2-1 victory. 15,606 spectators on a sunny August Saturday, 1982 saw a stirring win by:

Burridge; John Humphrey; John Pender; Bobby Coy; Geoff Palmer; Peter Daniel; Mick Matthews; David Wintersgill; Wayne Clarke; Billy Livingstone (Paul Butler); Mel Eves (2).

John Burridge was an ever-present in the Wolves side which marched straight back to Division One, yet promised only to deceive as it just as quickly screamed back down again, the momentum carrying a continuously-changing personnel ever downwards. But that decline would only feature Budgie for one season, a First Division term in which he once again demonstrated what a fine goalkeeper he is.

"I enjoyed it - I had tremendous rapport with the fans, winning the player-of-the-year trophy."

Certainly, few will forget the ebullient way with which the extrovert custodian would greet the faithful, roaring their approval behind his goal. Who could forget his acrobatics, the habit of walking across the pitch on his hands before games or the time he took to the arena dressed as Superman? Here was a true crowd-pleaser, a born-entertainer, but a man whose goalkeeping obsession made him such a formidable obstacle for the opposition even in some of Wolves' darker days.

"Graham Hawkins was a relaxed sort of guy, but Jim Barron worked me really hard. He's quite exceptional with the goalkeepers. My old mate Andy Gray, who I've always thought a lot of, was there, so it was good. Coming out of London we were able to afford a mansion in Tettenhall, even though we didn't really want to leave the big city."

Apart from a ten match spell in 1983-84, when Paul Bradshaw was recalled much to John's distress, Budgie was an automatic choice for Wolves. It was a shock to all around Molineux when he refused his new contract in the Summer of 1984 and was unavailable to go between the sticks for the commencement of the Docherty era.

"Charlie, I know my value. The same happened later at Southampton. If a club doesn't pay me what I'm worth, then I'll move. It's as simple as that.

"I went on loan to Derby, but I didn't want to go into the Third Division. I respected Arthur Cox, who is a great manager. They were offering me a lot of money and there were a lot of promises about who they were going to sign. But I've heard all that before.

"So I went to Sheffield United (for a cut-price £10,000), a club going up and certainly one step nearer the First Division. Arthur Cox fell out with me over that and has never let me forget it. As it happened, Derby got to the First before Sheffield, but I had three great years at Bramall Lane. We didn't win anything, but I played out of my skin for them.

"After that, Ian Porterfield, my manager at United, could have signed me for Aberdeen, but I decided to go to Southampton. The press made a lot about them trying to replace the Almighty Shilton with a Second Division man. But I had two exceptional years down there. In my opinion I kept them in the First Division. They had a lot of good young players, the Le Tissiers and Wallaces, but they weren't ready. I played out of my skin.

"Spurs and Chelsea came in for me, but Chris Nicholl wouldn't let me go. I'd have loved to have gone back to London, but I stayed. In my opinion I was completely and utterly let down. The Board were not prepared to pay me what I was worth, so I left."

And thence to Newcastle United and once more to the Second Division.

"I love it up here. They're the best club I've ever played for - by far. This is a football club. This is what it's all about. The whole area revolves around just one thing: the black-and-white. It's not that way at Wolves, at Sheffield, anywhere. They think they're fanatics in Liverpool and at Manchester United. But they're not - for them it's the glamour. But up here they come because it's their life. They've had it tough, but still they turn up."

John Burridge is quite clear about his future.

"We've opened a shop in Sunderland. My wife, Janet, is very astute. She can't just shut the door and make the dinner. But I have to stay in the game at some level - preferably as a manager. I'm my own person and I want to learn the trade. And I know I can do it.

"But, Charlie, I'm playing better than I've ever played. I'm far better now that I was at 28. I've kept myself utterly fit - I live for football."

I have no doubts in my mind that the incomparable Budgie will be around long after Peter Shilton. And the game will be that much the richer for it.

*

As Greavesie is wont to say, football is a funny old game. Before the 1990-91 season was played out Ossie Ardiles had taken the reins at St James' Park and John Burridge was once more a free agent, bound for Hibernian.

THE VOLUNTEER

"I was just happy to be in the team. I was too naive to be worried. Yes, I was nervous, but the season went like a dream. I couldn't have hoped to play that well. It didn't frustrate me particularly to be in a declining team - I honestly didn't understand the way that things were going at board level. I was quiet. I didn't say anything in team meetings. I would now, now that I've more confidence. It would have frustrated me now to have players in front of me that didn't really belong in a Wolverhampton Wanderers jersey."

Tim Flowers has come a long way from the raw youth that was pitched prematurely into the turmoil of Wolves' darkest days of decline. Only with the passing of time and the acquisition of the experience which is so critical to a fully-fledged goalkeeper, can Tim look back dispassionately at the days when, all too often, it seemed to most of us that it was a plucky 17-year-old against the rest at Molineux.

It's difficult to grasp the fact that Flowers is still in the first flush of youth.

Tim Flowers was born in Kenilworth on 3rd February , 1967. As a schoolboy he liked to play centre-forward -"everyone likes to score!" - but his life was changed after spotting an advert in the local paper.

"Some bloke was starting a Sunday League team in Coventry, so I went along for a trial. He asked for keepers, but none of the 30 or 40 lads stepped forward. It was really embarrassing, so my dad urged me to volunteer. I went on to play for that under-15's team, Coventry Dynamo, for five or six years in the Mid-Warwickshire League and then the Coventry Minor League. The club was affiliated to Coventry Sporting and became their youth team.

"By now, though, I was training with the Wolves, so I had to join their nursery team in Coventry called Parkstone United. I was still at Kenilworth School, where my teacher wouldn't let me play in goal. So I played at centre-half alongside Graham Rodger!"

Tim left school with 4 'O' levels to become an apprentice at Molineux. He had been training with Wolves since the age of 13 after being invited by John Hanna.

"I used to go between seven and nine on a Thursday evening for training by Dave Wagstaffe and Roy Pritchard. Dad used to take me over after school - I was exhausted by the time I got home to Kenilworth afterwards.

"In the school holidays I was always up there training at Cosford, learning what the apprentices did."

Flowers was thrilled when Graham Hawkins signed him alongside Rodger as a 15-year-old. One of his first jobs was to look after John Burridge's kit.

"I got tremendous help from Budgie. He's so dedicated. He'd give me gloves and jerseys and so on. Jim Barron did quite a bit with me - but Budgie would have me back in the afternoons working with him. He'd need help to get through his routines and, when he was tired, I'd go in goal."

Another major influence on Flowers' Molineux upbringing was Youth Coach Frank Upton.

"Frank is an absolutely brilliant man. He was very much a disciplinarian, but he had a heart of gold. That's so important for kids. He was like a second father. I couldn't believe it when they sacked him, the same day as Jim Barron. He'd taken boys and made them into men."

Indeed Upton had forged a formidable collection of youth players good enough to win the Midland Youth Cup. Apart from Flowers and his friend Graham Rodger (striker John Hathaway was another pal), defenders Paul Shipley and Steve Thomas also emerged through the Parkstone stable. All four were on duty one miserable night in November 1982 when Tim had the misfortune to pick the ball four times from his goal on his Central League debut against Blackpool. He had stepped in for ex-Northampton keeper Andy Poole, who was understudy to Burridge. On an evening when Dave Bamber struck a hattrick in the 4-0 Molineux rout, Wolves fielded:

Flowers; Shipley; Mark Bromley; Rodger; Thomas; Stephen Pugh (sub Steve Devine); David Wintersgill; Jonathan Laws; Martin Bayly; Gordon Miller; Billy Livingstone.

Tim Flowers was called upon for seven second team games the following season, as giants Burridge and Paul Bradshaw haggled over the senior billing. He won for himself England Youth honours, too. Useful experience was forthcoming on Wanderers' mid-season dart to Kuwait, where Tim enjoyed a goalless appearance against their National team. He could not have expected that just six months later, hours after signing full professional forms, he'd be playing first team football for real.

"Paul Bradshaw had gone. John had contract problems - that's it about Budgie: once he's finished his contract and if he doesn't like the new one, he packs his boots and he's off. I was the only one left."

New manager Tommy Docherty had no option but to give young Flowers his chance. He did well in the 2-2 draw with Sheffield United, impressing the 14,908 crowd, and earning star billing, with his immaculate handling and sharpness off the line. The team was

Flowers; John Humphrey; Geoff Palmer; Paul Dougherty; John Pender; Alan Dodd (1); Alan Ainscow (Derek Ryan); Tony Evans; Tommy Langley (1); Ian Cartwright; Paul Butler.

Tim missed just four games that season, which was a personal (if not collective) triumph. He 'walked' the supporters' player of the season trophy, having comfortably replaced Burridge in the affections of the faithful who knew promise when they saw it. The Midland Sportswriters made Tim their Young Player of the Year.

"Tommy Docherty? He was great for me. He stuck by me - treated me as his own lad. Every time I made a mistake he'd call me in, reassure me. He bulled me up in the press, made a good name for me that season."

Wolves' relegation to the Third Division could scarcely be laid at the door of their young custodian. The next season, however, was an anticlimax for Tim, who alternated with Scott Barrett in the team.

"I couldn't maintain the form of the previous season. Scott and I had a good relationship - there was never any enemy-type feeling. I've never had that with any colleague. That sort of attitude is just stupid."

By the end of March, 1986 Barrett had wrested the position for himself, restricting Flowers to the frustration of the Central League side.

"It was rumoured that Southampton's Tony Barton was watching me. Then Sammy Chapman asked me whether I'd like to train down there with Peter Shilton. On the Monday I was met on the motorway by Brian Truscott, Saints' secretary, and I started work as soon as he got me there. With Shilton, it was training like I'd never known before. It hit me how unfit I really was: I was knackered and in bed by nine o'clock."

Flowers was frustrated, then, to be recalled by Wolves within the week after Barrett had been injured. He played out Wolves' third successive relegation season before signing for Southampton at a fee of £70,000.

"I was actually in Crete when the story broke that I'd been transferred: Dad telegrammed to tell me! I actually put pen to paper when I got home!

"Peter Shilton was a great help to me. At first his training regimes were alien to me, but once I understood and appreciated their purpose I found them amazing. My game improved so much just through greater fitness in the first few months."

Flowers played in the pre-season programme of friendlies in 1986, including the 4-1 victory over Benfica, though Shilts returned from World Cup duty for the opening Division One game with Queen's Park Rangers. Injury to the England keeper, however, gave Tim his big chance at Old Trafford.

"They did us five. Charlie, I didn't know what hit me. I was stunned when I came out. The noise was unreal. They had a fair team, of course - Strachan and so on. But I thought, what am I doing here?!

"Villa Park, Anfield - you don't half learn a lot from playing these places. I've learned to control the butterflies. It's about state of mind. At Wolves it was a case of 'how many can we keep it down to?'

"That's a rubbish attitude. I've developed physically, but I've improved mentally as well. You learn motivation: you're GOING to win."

After a couple of games in the first team, Tim stepped down again for Shilton. And then, ironically, Southampton secured Eric Nixon on loan to deputise for the senior man. With Swindon's Fraser Digby suspended, Lou Macari summonsed Tim to fill the breach on loan, useful experience for the young keeper after a lengthy spell in the Football Combination.

With Shilton injured again, however, Flowers had a run of seven games at the end of the term, only to miss out on the final game at Coventry.

"I was desperate to play in that one for obvious reasons. I was that disappointed - we hadn't lost a match in my run."

Nevertheless, Tim Flowers had obviously done enough to convince manager Chris Nicholl that he could afford to accept Derby's bid for Shilton, and the number one jersey was handed to the ex-Wolves man at the start of 1987-88. After nine League games, culminating in a 4-0 home defeat by Everton, and a shock League Cup dismissal by neighbours Bournemouth, Saints recruited a familiar face: John Burridge.

"Yes it was frustrating. But I've the utmost respect for Budgie. I like him as a person. His fitness is absolutely magnificent - if anything he trains harder than Shilts. Mentally and physically he's in tremendous shape. He may or may not be the best - but he THINKS he is, and that's how he keeps himself going. And who's to say he's wrong?"

Tim had another five game spell at The County Ground before returning to work with Budgie at The Dell. For two seasons he understudied the Cumbrian, before the peripatetic Budgie had flown again. Tim Flowers, by now capped three times for the England Under-21 side, was ready to stake his claim for keeps.

"At the beginning of 1989-90 it was make or break. Fortunately I got into the team."

And, despite the arrival of highly fancied Ian Andrews from Celtic as valued competition, Tim has established himself as first choice. Domestically he's well-settled in a new home near Winchester, to which he has taken wife Jane and daughter Emma Jane, born Christmas Eve, 1989. He's very much a family man, as you'd expect from someone whose own family have been such a tremendous influence, attending most of his games. At Wolverhampton he had, too, a second mum and dad in Jack and Olive Carr, with whom he lodged. To this day he still calls them up on a Friday evening.

His personal ambitions are clear:

"Of course I want to play for England - it's every player's ambition to represent his country. But I want to become a seasoned campaigner in the First Division - a week-in, week-outer. That's what Jimmy Case says - you need a mental toughness."

Tim Flowers has certainly had some outstanding tutors. There seems every reason to believe that in the future he may surpass all of them in personal achievement, allying as he does an innate ability with the desire to work hard and to succeed, urges enmeshed in a straightness and pleasantness of character. He pays tribute to some of those 'tutors':

"Shilton taught me a hell of a lot. But I've known Budgie for such a long time. He must've 'phoned Shilts and asked him what he's doing 'cos he was doing exactly the same sort of thing! That was a bonus for me: no new routines to learn! But I must say that Paul Bradshaw was a superb goalkeeper, capable of the most incredible saves. Whyever didn't he work as hard as Budgie?"

Tim Flowers won't fall into any trap of lethargy, for all his natural ability. He means to reach the top. Don't bet against it.

No relation - Tim and Ron Flowers

pro
uhlsport

NOT THE SON OF SAM

"Nobody could speak after that third game. I genuinely didn't realise just how great a thing it was - I was naive, I suppose. On balance, though, it was probably a good thing that it turned out that way: it made everyone realise how low the club had got."

It is tragic for any young footballer when his first steps on the game's ladder are taken in a match which signalled a club's lowest ebb. Pity then the goalkeeper in a three match 1986 F.A. Cup series against Chorley which saw Wolverhampton Wanderers unceremoniously dumped from the competition by a humble Northern Premier League side. In no way could the 18-year-old in question be blamed for that 3-0 defeat at Burnden Park: he merely had the misfortune of coinciding with a sequence of events totally beyond his control. In a just football world he would never have been forced into such traumatic circumstances. But then, the early football career of Vincent Bartram has been anything but typical.

Vince was born on the 7th August 1968 at Dudley Road Hospital in Smethwick. Like so many goalies he fancied himself as a centre-forward, but his earliest steps in the game were as a 12-year-old right back for White Lion Rangers, a pub team in Cannock.

"When the family moved back to live in Halesowen I tried to get into the school team at centre-forward, but could never manage it. In lunchtime kick arounds I would go into goal between the thrown-down jumpers and, when the team's keeper fancied himself as a winger, I went into goal for the school."

Vince was 13, it was Hagley R.C. School and his best mate was Darren Wassall, soon to become a promising defender at Nottingham Forest.

"I went through the ranks - school team, district side, Sunday football. Then a teacher at the school recruited me for Oldswinford from the Banks's League. They were just setting up an Under-15's side in the Walsall League, after which it was an under-18's side in the Birmingham Boys League. I played for them at 16 in the Reserves, before getting a couple of matches for the first team at the end of the season.

"One was against Bilston, an official of which club was Tony Painter, a Wolves scout. He spotted me, although his prime target was Neil Edwards. Come May Day Bank Holiday in 1985, Tim Flowers broke his wrist saving a penalty at Brighton. Scott Barrett was called into the first team - so they had nobody to play the following Saturday in the Intermediates. On the Friday I got a call from Chief Scout Sammy Chapman asking me if I fancied a game against Villa the next day. Villa had the likes of Gary Shaw and Mark Burke in their side, so I was delighted to keep a clean sheet in a 2-0 win at Castlecroft.

"When we got back to Molineux, Sammy asked 'on Thursday the youth team are going to Holland -would you like to go?' I got the school's permission and we went on to win the tournament. I saved two penalties in the shoot-out in the semi-final. 'We'll be in touch' said Sammy. 'Well, that's that' I remember thinking but, sure enough, Sammy (now acting manager) called pre-season to ask me to come down."

Wolves signed Vince, still at school, on the agreement that he came in for training on Wednesdays. Thus the adrenalin was pumping for the young keeper throughout the week, as he combined 'A' level studies at Hagley with learning his trade as a footballer.

"I never did get the 'A' levels: football just takes over. I'd suddenly get a call at school: 'we need you for the Reserves at Sunderland tonight'."

Vince had established something to fall back on with a dozen 'O' levels, but increasingly football was making more demands. As Flowers and Barrett successively picked up knocks, young Bartram was summonsed from his Stourbridge home to ply his trade in a raw Central League side for whom only the likes of Mike Coady and Peter Zelem could offer any degree of defensive experience. 0-5 at Rotherham, 0-4 to Grimsby, 0-4 at Roker, 0-7 against Notts County at Molineux: it was a baptism of hellfire for young Vince. He kept his head high, however, and thrived on the challenge and the opportunity to work at his game with a famous professional club, albeit one in serious decline.

Vince Bartram couldn't have imagined that, within a very few short months, he'd start a season as first choice keeper.

"I didn't ever think about playing in the first team. Things just happened. I wasn't nervous. The whole thing built up for weeks during the summer."

Tim Flowers had signed for Southampton. Scott Barrett injured his knee on the first day of pre-season training. Vince was the only keeper left. Acting boss Brian Little had no choice but to pitch the raw custodian into the fray against Cambridge.

"To be honest I think that, if Brian had his time over again, he'd have gone straightaway for someone on loan. But the club was in such a low state."

In fact it seemed almost certain at one point that the financial crisis would mean that Wolves wouldn't be in a position to start the term at all, so Mr Little had no option but to field the players already at his disposal. 6,016 hardy souls turned up at Molineux on 23rd August 1986 to herald the start of the Homden/Harris/Gallagher era and to witness a skinny young man in a baggy green sweater pluckily bow-in for their battered heroes. Cambridge won 2-1.

"In the first half I thought I did O.K. Then in the second I've made a good save but the ball has come back off a post, hit an attacker and the ref's for some reason given a corner from which they score. We equalised, but then in the last minute I thought I was left stranded by a defender. That was that - I won't mention his name!"

In fact it was Matt Hellin, playing his solitary game for the club. Otherwise Wolves fielded

Bartram; Darren Oldroyd; David Barnes; Floyd Streete; Peter Zelem (1); Hellin; Matt Forman; Mickey Holmes; Andy Mutch; Neil Edwards; Jon Purdie.

On the Tuesday it was the mixture as before, this time in the Littlewoods (League) Cup. Wolves were drawing 1-1 with Lincoln with five minutes to go, when Vince was defeated from 20 yards by a scorcher into the top corner.

"Next day Brian Little explained that he was getting Eric Nixon in on loan. He was really good about it: it really took the pressure off. Brian explained that I was still needed for the second leg match at Lincoln and I went on to keep a clean sheet.

"Eric was no real help to me directly - but I could see the sort of standards that I had to achieve by watching him. I'd worked with Tim Flowers a couple of times - but he never really helped me as such. He was doing it for himself - remember, he was only young too. The first person who really helped me was Mark Kendall, who was great."

But the burly Welshman at that stage was still trying to get away from Somerton Park. And with Nixon ruled out of cup fixtures and Barrett not fully recovered from injury, new manager Graham Turner once more turned to young Bartram when faced with the apparently easy task of removing Chorley from the F.A. Cup.

How Wolves failed to dispose of the Lancashire side in the first replay at Molineux on November 15th, 1986 will remain as one of life's great mysteries. As Vince recalls

'I got soaking wet. And their goal was yards offside."

Indeed, that's the way it seemed to all 4,790 spectators as Paul Moss was found completely unmarked and a good five yards adrift of the last Wolves defender. As Vince came out, the darting striker had a straightforward job of lifting the ball over the keeper's head for an undeserved equaliser to Forman's stunning opener. After that Bartram could only stand frustrated as his forwards were repeatedly thwarted by his opposite number Ian Senior. Even so, bar some weak clearances in the face of an extreme wind, Bartram availed himself extremely well, thrilling the crowd with one splendid catch of a rasping, slippy ball.

Thence to Burnden and the agony of a tie looted by Chorley's Magpies. For Vince it was his last senior opportunity before a prolonged chance to "learn the game" in the less exposed environs of reserve team soccer. He acknowledges the help of several.

"When Mark Kendall came at Christmas 1986 it was just a case of us talking about my game. Then in training he'd stand behind the goal and comment on my style. We'd talk over my matches the day after -'this is what I did, what would you have done?'

"Then Mark suggested that Peter Williams, who'd been coaching the keepers at the School of Excellence, come in and work with us on Monday afternoons. Now we have Eric Steele, of whom I can't speak highly enough: he's helped my game ten-fold.

"I used to think that goalkeeping was just a case of standing between the sticks and keeping it out. But talking to experienced guys teaches you that it's an art. The Boss likes experienced goalkeepers: I have to hold my hands up and admit that I'm still very young and have a lot to learn. But every game I play is experience, even in the Reserves. Even in that team, when I started it was playing in the Midland Intermediate League. Then we've gone Midland Senior, Pontins Division Two and now Pontins Division One. Each year it's been a better standard."

Early in 1990, Vince got the chance to pick up critical experience in the Third Division at Blackpool.

"We'd had an easy Friday morning on the car park at Molineux and I'd gone home to lunch. I was met by Grandad who told me that they were after me at the ground. The Boss said that Blackpool wanted me on loan for a month as cover for Steve McIlhargey who'd had 50 stitches in a ripped mouth. They were playing at Rotherham next day. Looking at the paper I saw that Rotherham were top of the division! I dashed to Molineux and signed the forms which were faxed off to get me registered in time.

"Next morning I met up with Blackpool's assistant manager Mick Jones at Trowell Services on the M1, met my team mates for the first time at 12.30 and we kicked off at 3.00. The first thing I did was to pick the ball out of the net! But then I had a couple of good saves and took all the crosses, being big and strong. In the second half, with the wind behind me, I got in some massive kicks so they were impressed with that! We drew 1-1."

Vince kept his place until the cup tie with Bolton, transmitted on television in view of its historic connections with the Matthews final of 1953. Graham Turner didn't want Vince cup-tied, so it was back to base.

"The following Thursday, however, Keith Pearson, the Wolves secretary, told me that I was off again to the seaside. I thought he was joking, but sure enough Steve had a groin strain and they reckoned the competition was good for him anyway. There was Steve and I - sharing a room before the match at Cardiff, lying there wondering who was going to get the nod. Luckily I got in and Steve came back for the cup.

"I enjoyed it - it's such a shame Blackpool went down. They are a great set of lads - almost as good as the Wolves, which is saying something."

Vince and I were chatting in his parents' immaculate home in Stourbridge, the family dog snoring contentedly under the table. Perhaps my timing could have been better, Mike Stowell's expensive arrival having been announced that very day. Bartram was philosophical about the situation, particularly after a two season spell away from first team consideration in which time Stowell, Roger Hansbury and Steele were brought in as temporary cover for the ailing Kendall and Tony Lange became the first of Turner's expensive custodial purchases.

"It's a kick in the teeth - of course it is. Obviously I'd like to get into the first team. And if the circumstances arise then I hope they'll have faith in me. But Mr Turner simply believes that his keepers should have experience. He's told me that he thinks I'll become a good keeper and that I need to keep learning the trade and get that experience. If people like that keep being straight with you it can't be a bad thing, can it?"

Vince Bartram has already learned a great deal. Intriguingly he considers his best feature to be his kick. Playing before a home crowd that seems to determine a goalkeeper's worth from the ability to field crosses, I enquired of Vince how he feels he rates in this regard:

"It's probably the most difficult part of the job, needing skill, bravery and judgement. One tournament in France, I recall coming for them right on the edge of the box. But on the Continent you can do that - you call and they just let you come. In England it's different. They deliberately impede you, cover your eyes, hold your arms - anything to make life difficult. But if you're good at taking crosses then you make your team look good.

"The sort of treatment Mark Kendall got from some of the crowd does get on your mind. A lot of people think they know about goalkeeping. But it's more than saving shots. Folk don't realise the little intricacies. Fans don't notice, for instance, the talking that a keeper does. Mark Kendall was great at that. When I first came to the Wolves I didn't talk enough. Then they told me that I was 'droning', that there was no variation in the tone of my calling. Different situations, different urgencies need a change of tone.

"And it's a different game these days. Dad is always telling me about the old players, but you can't really compare them with today's. See how much room they used to give Matthews and then see how many men they set on Maradonna. Balls are much lighter; players shoot more powerfully; the ball swerves and dips more.

"Little things. When I first played in a match with a brand new ball I found that it was ever so slippery. Your gloves don't grip for five minutes. It may sound trivial, but you have to be doubly careful at the start."

When he's not in action himself, Vince is a regular watcher of the game. In fact he can still be seen following the fortunes of his boyhood heroes, West Bromwich Albion! He hasn't made a particular study of goalkeepers, though lists Shilton, Southall and Coton as the ones he most admires. He is strictly no relation to the legendary Sam ("I wish I had a pound for every time I've been asked - but we do have the book about him!"). When not involved in soccer, Vince plays golf off a handicap of 20.

It's over six years ago that Vince Bartram first burst onto the Molineux senior scene. Tall, immaculately groomed, intelligent and refreshingly personable, it is easy to see how he could comfortably follow his father into accountancy. Before that, however, there is a lot of goalkeeping to get out of his skin. He's on the upward slope of the learning curve - another Bartram goalkeeping great may be in the making.

Events have a habit of moving on apace in football. 1990-91 saw loan spells for Vince at Cheltenham (under Jim Barron) and at his beloved Hawthorns. Then, of course, with Mike Stowell injured and Tony Lange unable to make the impact he would have wished, once more the youngster was called upon to acquit himself well.

With veteran Gerry Peyton moving to Everton as cover for Neville Southall, Bouremouth came in search of a 'young pretender' and happily wrote a cheque for £65,000 in July 1991 for Bartram.

umbro
WOLVES

THE LATE STARTER

"I simply walked into Maine Road one Friday afternoon and asked Ken Barnes for a trial. I thought 'well, they can only say no'. In fact on the Tuesday they gave me a game against Barnsley Reserves and Billy McNeill signed me fulltime on a six months contract. Mostly I played Central League games, but after a testimonial against Stockport they gave me a year."

It was 1984. Eric Nixon was approaching his 22nd birthday and he was thrilled to have joined his boyhood heroes, Manchester City, as reserve to Alex Williams. His footballing career up until then had been in relative obscurity. At last he had the opportunity to show what he was worth.

Eric was born on the 4th October 1962 at Harpur Hay in Manchester. He wasn't always a goalkeeper.

"I was a centre-forward in a Sunday league team and went for a trial for Manchester Boys at the age of eleven. Too many strikers had turned up so, being a big lad, I had a bash in goal. It went well. From then on I'd play in goal on a Saturday and on a Sunday morning and centre-forward on a Sunday afternoon!

"When I left school I worked for three years as an upholstery cutter and then did general labouring, car valeting - anything."

But Eric was getting increasingly devoted to his goalkeeping.

"I played for Anson Villa in the Cheshire League with my friend David 'Taffy' Jones, and then with St Christopher's, a church team. Taffy went to Curzon Ashton, so I joined him there. I was at Curzon for three years, before signing for City. The fee was £1,000."

For two seasons, Nixon had to be content with second team football, but was relishing the chance to learn about the game from working alongside Alex Williams.

"But for Alex I wouldn't have made the grade. He inspired me. I wanted to be as good as him. Now I know I can be better. We were coached by the former England keeper Alan Hodgkinson, who did a tremendous amount of work with me. Believe me, it's a different life as a keeper going from semi-pro to fulltime. Hodgkinson gave me the ammo to play first division football."

Williams played the entire season 1984-1985 when City regained their first division status. However the following season his injuries gave Eric Nixon the opportunity for which he'd been patiently waiting and a debut against West Ham United at Maine Road.

"We drew 2-2 in front of over 25,000 and my relatives forgot about me after the game, so I had to walk home in the rain! On the following Wednesday we beat Bury in the Milk Cup and things went well, so Billy McNeill kept me in for the rest of the season."

Nixon, however, patently did not get along with McNeill, who brought in various loan signings in preference to the young giant. Thus the likes of Barry Siddall, Bobby Mimms and, indeed, Mike Stowell came in before McNeill splashed out over £100,000 for Perry Suckling.

"We went away on tour to the States and to Sweden and I felt I'd done enough to keep my place, but he obviously wasn't going to play the local lad when he'd paid all that money for Perry."

So Eric Nixon embarked on his own series of loan transfers which gave him the opportunity to become the only man ever to keep goal in all four divisions in a single season.

"Brian Little phoned up from Wolves asking for a keeper and City were going to send Steve Crompton. But Brian said he wanted someone more experienced, so I was happy to go down. I loved it. After a month Little was sacked, but I stayed on for two months under Graham Turner. Graham enquired two or three times about me staying permanently, but Billy McNeill wasn't prepared to sell. I would have been thrilled to stay. In fact, before I signed for Tranmere, I did let Mr Turner know that I was available, but nothing came of it.

"I stayed with Jack and Olive Carr, who were smashing. When I first went to Wolves the club was going nowhere, but we all seemed to work well together and gradually the results and the crowds started coming. I palled on especially with Andy Mutch, 'Digger Barnes' and Keith Lockhart - but everyone treated me great. Tell me - have they still got that photograph of me on the wall? I look like a convict!"

Nixon's debut for Wolves came at Aldershot on 30th August 1986. Goals from Lockhart and Mutch brought Wolves a 2-1 victory:

Eric Nixon; Darren Oldroyd; Nicky Clarke; Floyd Streete (Roger Eli); Peter Zelem; Steve Stoutt; Keith Lockhart; Mick Holmes; Andy Mutch; Derek Ryan; Jon Purdie.

Jim Barron was coaching the Wolves keepers at the time, and Eric recalls fondly the excellent workouts he enjoyed with Vince Bartram and Scott Barrett - "there was no animosity".

"At Wolves I felt I was wanted - after all they had ASKED for me. It was the same at the other clubs I joined on loan, whereas at City I was just another keeper, just a number.

"I enjoyed all my loan spells - except Bradford City where I just didn't play as well as I can. But when I came back from there, Southampton wanted me. I really liked it at The Dell, working with Peter Shilton who is everything they say about him. We worked really hard - him, me, Phil Kite and the youngsters, too.

"In fact I've had bits and pieces off some of the best keepers - for, after Southampton, I went with Harry Gregg to Carlisle. But each time I had to come back to City to be second."

Finally it was a loan spell to Tranmere Rovers which paved the way for Eric Nixon's bright new future.

"We did really well in the Mercantile Credit tournament at Wembley, you'll remember. Talking to Johnny King and looking around me - it was obvious that Tranmere were going places. And I thought, well if I join them they really will go places.

"Look. In no way am I conceited. No way am I a bighead, I am simply confident in my own ability. As a goalkeeper you have to be, otherwise you're nothing. As far as I'm concerned I'm the best in the League. One day I'll play for England."

It seems that his manager shares his belief, King telling me that "Eric can be top of the poll". His fellow professionals certainly have a high regard for Nixon, voting him in successive seasons best keeper in Division Four and Division Three.

Unsurprisingly, Eric Nixon signed for Tranmere at a fee of £60,000 in 1988.

"I've loved every minute of it. It's a great club, with great people, great facilities. Yes, all that business in the Summer of 1990 with Swindon was a bit irritating. But we've taken it with a pinch of salt. We'll get promoted the right way - everyone on Merseyside knows that. We're big enough just to get on with it. Teams nowadays are scared to come to Prenton Park."

1989-90 saw Tranmere at Wembley twice - for the unsuccessful play-offs, but also for that Leyland-Daf victory over Bristol Rovers.

"Tremendous - I'd been with City for the Full Members against Chelsea, but didn't do particularly well in the 5-4 defeat. This time I made sure I was going to take in every moment. Thankfully, everything went well."

It was a scorching first day in August 1990 when I met up with Eric at Tranmere's superb Valley Road training complex in Birkenhead. He is a towering figure, dressed on this occasion in just a pair of shorts, huge muscles decorated by a discrete tattooed rose on the upper right arm and a deep bronzed tan. Clearly he is ultra-fit - an athleticism honed by regular Thursday sessions at Everton's Belfield training ground.

"Jim Barron comes up to take the Everton, Tranmere and sometimes Wrexham keepers. It's the perfect end to the week's training. Neville Southall is superb - he may be acclaimed as the best in the world, but he just mucks in like a youth team keeper. I worked with Mick Stowell a lot too, obviously.

"I admire Neville greatly - as I did Joe Corrigan, who people were always slaughtering, but he showed them all in the end. Another I rate but have never really met is Tony Coton.

"In terms of the help I've had I must mention Hodgkinson and Barron, but especially my old friend 'Taffy' Jones. Every Summer we go out on the field behind his home and train really hard. I'm reaping the benefits now.

"I've signed a new two year contract for Tranmere - but I want to be a first division goalkeeper. I KNOW I have the ability. First, though, I want to do what Bully has done - play for England"

With Shilton out of the way, don't bet against that. Eric Nixon has the determination, the self-belief and the ability. He simply needs the right people to sit up and take notice.

1990-91 saw Nixon's Tranmere at Wembley twice more. This time it was defeat in the Freight Rover, but most crucially a triumph in the play-offs. The Second Division beckoned.

KENDO

The players' lounge was humming with post-victory excitement. Wolves had just defeated top club Leeds United by a solitary goal and the prospect of joining the Yorkshiremen in the 1990 promotion push was still very much on the cards.

One by one the players, wearing that moist just-showered look, entered to meet up with colleagues, friends and admirers and gratefully receive the cans of Carling Black Label or glasses of coke or lemonade thrust into their hands.

One of the last to appear through the door was Mark Kendall. He didn't so much walk into the room as bounce. One got the impression that the manner of his entrance would have been identical no matter what the scoreline had been. Wolves had, in fact, secured a notable win largely on the back of two stupendous saves from the burly Welshman. The second had been an astonishing leap to punch over a thunderous close range header from Lee Chapman, a save which almost warranted a re-examination of Newton's Laws of Gravity.

The keeper, popular with the majority, cheerfuly signed assorted scraps of paper, programmes and autograph books, grabbed a couple of cans of Tennent's Pilsner and ushered me out onto the sadly redundant Waterloo Road terracing.

'Well played, Mark' I enthused, a masterpiece of understatement.

"Thanks - not at all bad, was it?" came the reply, "that's a point proved, don't you think?"

A gleam flashed through his eyes. For almost a season, scattered abuse had been hurled at Kendall from those who were less appreciative of the keeper's efforts than they might have been. Did the boo-boys perturb him, I wondered?

"Look. If you try to give 110% to the game and you're honest with yourself, then yes, it does worry you. If you had a bad attitude and couldn't care less, then it might not. But it doesn't matter who you are or what you do, there'll always be someone that doesn't like you. The important thing is to please the manager!"

As we leaned over a barrier in the mellow glow of the early evening sun shining across a deserted Molineux, Kendall's determination and love of his profession were transparent.

"I'm 31, but I want to continue playing for as long as my body and spirit will allow - there's no substitute for playing. After all this time in the game there's not much new. Training, for instance, gets repetitive. So enthusiasm is the main thing and at the moment I enjoy the game very much."

Off the field, Kendall seldom seems to be without a grin on that distinctive moustachioed face. But the eyes beam defiance when he tells me

"People seem to have been writing me off as a player since I was eleven. They've always tried to push me aside. I won't let people do that to me. I've always been able to prove a point to people."

And the statistics live up to that. Mark Kendall joined up with Wolves when they were an unspectacular middle-of-the-road Fourth Division outfit. As we spoke after that Leeds game they were seventh in Division Two.

"We haven't lost many games, have we? And there've been plenty of clean sheets!"

Kendall is a wisecracker, a man who thrives on rapport with the crowd. But he takes his job seriously as you would expect from a bloke for whom defending a goalmouth has been life for over twenty years.

Born in Blackwood, deep in the Welsh Valleys, on 20th September 1958, Kendall attended a rugby playing grammar school but, faced with a choice of pursuing the handling code for his school or soccer for Pengam Boys Club, he chose the latter. At first he was a centre-half, but when their goalkeeper fell off a playground roundabout, Mark made the transition to keeper. He was twelve.

"The only soccer I watched was on television, with Spurs being my favourite team."

You can imagine how excited he was, then, to have Tottenham scout him out and for the legendary Bill Nicholson to sign him on schoolboy forms in 1974. Terry Neill secured him as an apprentice in April 1975 after Welsh Schoolboy honours had been earned.

"Spurs had plenty of good goalkeepers then, with Pat Jennings probably the best in the world at the time. No, I didn't have a lot to do with him - he is a very quiet man. You could tell him your problems and he was a great help then. But he never forced his opinions on anyone. What a superb presence he had, though."

Kendall found himself sixth choice on his arrival at White Hart Lane, with Barry Daines and Terry Lee as well as two young pros barring the way in the pecking order behind Jennings.

"Then they got rid of the two other youngsters, Pat was called up for the home internationals and so I was chosen to go as number two to Dainesy on the club's world tour. What a thrill! I was seventeen, had never flown before and there I was off to Canada, the States, Fiji, New Zealand and Australia."

In July 1976 Kendall signed up as a full-time pro and found himself playing the occasional Football Combination game for Spurs' Reserves. Daines was esconced in the first team as replacement for Jennings, whose transfer to neighbours Arsenal stupefied the Tottenham diehards. Daines was an ever-present in the side which restored the club's First Division status in 1977-78, but by November of the following term it was time for young Kendall to be given his head.

"Dainesy had gout! We went to Norwich, drew two-each and I learned a very quick lesson.In the 92nd minute (!) Martin Peters was waiting to take a free-kick and spotted that I'd taken my eye off the ball to line up the wall. He curled it straight in."

The chirpy youngster kept his place, however, until Easter, the high spot being an F.A. Cup quarter final appearance against Manchester United. He won an Under-21 cap for his country, too, against Scotland at a time when Glan Letheren and Martin Thomas were also in competition for the principality's yellow jersey.

For his club side, Kendall was rubbing shoulders with the likes of Steve Perryman, Osvaldo Ardiles and Ricky Villa. He ran up a total of 29 First Division appearances.

"They were 29 more than I expected, what with the turnover in apprentices and such like, and me just a young lad up from the valleys. To this day, every game I play is a bonus. It's wonderful to do a job that you always dreamed of doing."

Kendall didn't always see eye-to-eye with Keith Burkinshaw, the third 'gaffer' of his White Hart Lane career, who saw the need to invest a substantial sum in Milija Aleksic from Luton, sometime Stafford Rangers custodian. It meant a tripartite competition for the senior slot between Kendall, Daines and the new man with the unpronouncable name.

"I thought I'd done well enough for the club at 19, not having cost them a penny. A game every other week in the second team was no use to me."

In December 1979, then, the bags were packed and Kendall travelled to Chesterfield for a loan spell in the town best associated with goalkeeping excellence. His nine match spell included a solitary defeat as he assisted the Spireites to fourth spot in the Third Division. Then it was back to base. In September 1980 a £45,000 bid took Mark to Newport County, the club nearest to home.

"It seemed to me that Somerton Park was a good place to be at the time. I'd have first team football in a side competing for European Cup honours."

For sure, County had a respectable side in the Third Division, with Kendall's colleagues including Tommy Tynan, John Aldridge and future Wolves friend Nigel Vaughan.

"It really looked as though success could be a possibility. Financially, though, our backs were against the wall. I was there seven long years and never got the sniff of a move. For me it was like Colditz. I tried everything to get out - even a bloody wooden horse! And then for some reason or other they dropped me at Christmas in 1986, giving Roger Freestone (later to join Chelsea) his chance. On the Monday I was told that Wolves had been on the 'phone, wanted me on loan. The rest, as they say, is history!

"To be frank I was surprised that Newport let me go. Of course I'd heard all about what had happened at Wolverhampton, about the Bhattis and so on. I wondered what I was getting myelf into. But Wolves have such a history. I'm just glad that I've been a part of bringing them back up."

Kendall's debut for Wolves came on a chilly and damp Thursday, New Year's Day 1987. Despite a sterling opener for the new man who impressed with his vociferous organisation of the defence and superb drop-kick and thrown distribution, Wanderers succumbed 0-3 to Peterborough. Wolves' team read:

Kendall; Steve Stoutt; Nicky Clarke; Barry Powell; Chris Brindley; Ally Robertson; Jon Purdie; Andy Thompson (Neil Edwards); Steve Bull; Andy Mutch; Matt Forman.

The next three games saw clean sheets kept by the 5ft 11in Welshman and Wolves had turned a corner. By the season's end a £40,000 transfer had secured the new keeper and 15 out of 26 games had seen Mark repel all-comers, only for Wolves to miss out in the playoff's to Aldershot, inclusive of Mr Tony Lange.

Manager Graham Turner had proved what a shrewd judge of character he is, with Kendall's cockiness inspiring the young team. The next two seasons saw successive championships, Mark, meanwhile, had developed quite a rapport with the crowd and, for a long while, he seemed to be everyone's darling.

"I try to play football with a smile on my face. Too many players seem not to. Gone are the days of the clown prince, of the Len Shackletons and suchlike. It's so difficult these days, the way games are policed. So many things can be construed as inciting crowd incidents.

"But I do try to be entertaining. I won't go overboard to the detriment of the game, of course. But spectators do pay to be a part of what's going on on the park. It's pure theatre. Yet a small minority seem to take the way I behave as an affront."

Unsurprisingly and unhesitatingly Kendall cites 1988's Sherpa Van triumph at Wembley as the highspot of his time at Wolves.

"Just being in the game for so long with no measurable success - and then walking out at Wembley to see all that gold, to lift the trophy, all the euphoria. It was wonderful - so, too, were the promotions!"

Mark Kendall admits to no real low spots in his time at Molineux, except perhaps the aforesaid defeat against Aldershot. The critics in the crowd who believed they saw weaknesses in the big man's game need to realise that he, like so many other players, is not knocked off his cheery perch that easily. Did not, though, the signing of Lange in the summer of '89 come as a shock?

"The manager obviously had to do something. My cartilage operation didn't take the first time around and so I needed another. Mr Turner could have found himself without a keeper. Tony's arrival was a spur for me. He was unlucky to lose his place so quickly. If you like, he was a scapegoat for the team when the results hadn't gone right. But I came back, things went well - and I proved my point."

'Kendo' took another sip from his can and gazed across the Molineux pitch.

"My contract is up in June. Yes, I would like to be a part of the Wanderers' future if the offer is right. I have a wife and children to consider. Perhap's I'll be able to change the opinion of the doubting 20% in the crowd. If not, then I'm quite prepared for a fresh challenge wherever I am offered one."

Clearly Mark was not anticipating the free transfer which his manager was about to hand him. It certainly didn't please him, but it did offer the chance to return to his native Wales with Swansea City.

As the evening closed in, I asked him to analyse his own goalkeeping and to indicate who had been the biggest influence on his career.

"Me! Seriously, I've had my heroes and my game is made up from little bits of each of them. My biggest strength is probably organising my defence - I've always been able to talk a load of crap! Really, though, defenders do like to know where they stand. Although my critics wouldn't have it, my strength used to be crosses. In the lower divisions they come in nice and high for you to come for. But higher up they are whipped in at pace with a curve on them. Those aren't so easy! That's why you don't see Shilton coming for them that often either!"

Kendall recognizes only too well the feature of his game that excites the most controversy. His detractors would do well to understand his motives for not attempting to come for every cross - and realise the worth of a keeper so adept at marshalling a defence to deal with the more awkward balls. Equally, even his harshest critic would be surprised to hear Kendall be so self-deprecating about his shot-stopping abilities.

"I've never considered myself a shot-stopper - I haven't really got the build for it!"

The numerous reflex saves with which the admittedly heavy keeper thwarted allcomers in Wolves' fine successes during his tenure defy that viewpoint.

Mark Kendall dreads the day when he won't be trotting onto the pitch to ply his favourite trade.

"I've got an H.G.V. licence, but I hope I don't have to use that! Whatever I do will have to be something I enjoy - as well as pay the bills!"

Mark Kendall's stay at Molineux stands the test of detailed statistical analysis. One trusts he will be remembered not as a player who suffered appalling abuse from a minority, but rather as a true character, an enthusiast, a crowd-pleaser and a truly competent keeper.

"Yes, Paul, I see it too"!

KEEPER IN A SUITCASE

Bob Wilson probably doesn't remember it, but as a young lad intent on being a goalkeeper, Roger Hansbury wrote to him at Highbury. To his credit, the Arsenal custodian wrote back, answering the plea for help. How ironic that the particular youngster in question achieved something which the great Wilson did not: he wore the senior number one jersey for Wolverhampton Wanderers.

Roger Hansbury was born in Barnsley on 26th January, 1955 and grew up as a fan of his local club:

"Aye... Roy Ironside, 'Spud' Murphy..."

As a 14-year-old at Worsborough High School his goalkeeping career began.

"It was the usual old story: the keeper was getting all the stick and got fed up with it, so I had a bash. It went alright."

'Alright', in fact, to the extent that he gained selection for Barnsley Boys and the Yorkshire side.

"I would play for the school on Saturdays mornings, dash home for fish and chips, then turn out for Worsborough in the afternoon. And I was in goal for a Sunday team as well for good measure!

"One of the apprentice professionals at Norwich City, Stephen Brown, came home for the weekend to see his family in Barnsley. He was watching Barnsley Boys with his dad and, when he got back to Carrow Road, told Ron Saunders about me. I was offered a trial and asked to sign as an apprentice. However, I was an associate schoolboy at Oakwell and we had to wait for a board meeting to release me so that I could join Norwich."

Under the strict disciplinarian Saunders, Hansbury developed apace and, after two years as an apprentice, he signed full-time pro terms in January 1973.

"To be frank I didn't really have a lot of dealings with Ron Saunders - I never played a first team game for him, for example. But the reason I am still playing today is down to the discipline which he instilled. He taught me to work hard at my game."

Under Terry Alcock, the youth and reserve coach, Hansbury progressed through the South East Counties League side into the Football Combination team. There was, nevertheless, a major obstacle barring further progression: the spectacular Kevin Keelan, one time fledgling under Nigel Sims at Villa Park, but subsequently veteran of over 600 games for The Canaries.

"Kevin was very good to me, but really we were totally different goalkeepers. He was a natural, whereas I had to work really hard at everything I did. He taught me a lot, though."

I asked Roger about his first team debut for Norwich. His answer astounded me.

"I can't remember! You'll have to look that up in Rothman's! I simply don't recall games I've played. Ask me to name players in a side in the First Division at the moment and I'll be struggling. I love playing the game - but statistics? No.

"I do know, however, that John Bond was the manager by that time. John had a lot of faith in my ability -more than I had myself, in fact. Perhaps if I'd shared his faith I'd have risen to greater heights."

Keelan was certainly proving an immovable feast in the Carrow Road goalmouth, restricting Hansbury's opportunities to shine in the senior side. A spell of jaundice contracted on holiday in Spain didn't help, keeping Roger our of the game for six months. Bond realised that his young reserve, by now being pushed from the rear by the diminutive Clive Baker, needed to gain more League experience. Thus came the first of Roger's loan spells which have made him the veritable peripatetic last-liner.

"I went to Bolton Wanderers as second to Jim McDonagh, but I couldn't shift him either. Back at Norwich, Fred Davies had arrived on the coaching staff. My career took off. Fred concentrated on the keepers and he had a huge influence on me. He's also a very nice man."

Next stop for the suitcase was Cambridge United in November 1977 under Ron Atkinson.

"I enjoyed that. We got promoted from the Third. Brendan Batson was skipper, there was George Reilly and Floyd Streete. Oh and a big blond centre-forward - was it Bailey?"

I refreshed his memory about Alan Biley.

"That was it! Anyway it was a great time at Cambridge - Ron Atkinson made training so enjoyable, it was a pleasure to go into work."

Loan spell number three was to Orient the following season.

"Sorry, I don't recall who the manager was and who the senior keeper was."

In fact Jimmy Bloomfield was in the chair, and that fine custodian John Jackson kept Hansbury out of the side. It was soon back to base.

In over ten years at Carrow Road, Roger had ammassed 78 League appearances, plus the 11 for Cambridge. More would undoubtedly have materialised had it not been for the jaundice and an ankle broken pre-season when Roger was in pole position.

"I was really looking forward to starting off as first choice keeper. But because of my injury, they had to

recall Kevin Keelan from the States. I could never shake him off!"

Before long, Roger decided it was time to seek a new challenge.

"John Bond had left and his replacement, Ken Brown, felt he needed to replace me with Chris Woods. Ken didn't want me to go, but I felt that I should have been at the top of my career. Reserve team football was no good to me at the time.

"Bobby Moore telephoned to enquire whether I'd like to join him in Hong Kong. I had a two month trial with Eastern Athletic Club and actually stayed for two years. It was great, playing alongside the likes of Tommy Hutchison, Charlie George, Barry Daines, Barry Powell."

So why come back?

"You think the grass is always greener back home, don't you? I thought I was missing out by not being in English football. Looking back, it was a mistake to return. I'm enjoying life again now - but things didn't work out for me on coming back to Burnley."

John Bond re-signed his prodigy in 1983 - "John was like a father to me in football" - and Hansbury gave him and his successor John Benson (also ex-Norwich) good service in two Third Division seasons. Unfortunately, the latter coincided with relegation and, with Joe Neenan ready for his chance at Turf Moor, Roger was on his way again.

"I'd had talks with Frank Clark (a lovely fella) at Orient and they offered me a contract. But Frank advised me to look at the house market before I signed. After a couple of hours in which we realised that the prices were astronomical, I went back to say that I wouldn't be putting pen to paper! I'll always appreciate Frank Clark's honesty."

So Roger signed for another of his 'old' clubs, Cambridge, who now had Ken Shellito at the helm.

"No regrets going back - Cambridge are a great little club. Their training facilities are excellent. I've only fond memories of them."

Hansbury played in 37 of Cambridge's Fourth Division games in a sorry season when the club finished just two places off the bottom.

"Cambridge were in financial trouble. Once more John Bond came in for me - by now he was at Birmingham. To be honest, I didn't want to go to St Andrews, just as reserve to David Seaman. But Birmingham were struggling in the First. John pointed out that if they stayed up, then I'd only be one step away from a First Division spot. If they got relegated, then he'd be forced to sell Seaman and I'd be in anyway. That is of course what happened - but, after a season, Gary Pendrey took over as manager. He reckoned he needed a change of 'keeper! In came Tony Godden, out went I on loan to Sheffield United!"

One-time Wolf Peter Withe made the reverse trip and the extraordinary happening occurred of Hansbury keeping goal for The Blades against his paymasters and Withe scoring both goals against him in a 0-2 defeat!

By New Year 1988, however, Hansbury had ousted Godden. Soon, though, more competition had arrived, in the guise of Welshman Martin Thomas, a keeper who at times Wolves have not been ashamed to express interest in. After just three first team opportunities as third-choice in 1988-1989, Roger was delighted to get an unexpected call from Wolves' manager Graham Turner in March 1989. Mark Kendall had finally succumbed to a long-standing injury and Turner had recruited Mike Stowell from Everton as a loan replacement. The tall blond Lancastrian, however, was cup-tied for the Sherpa Van Trophy games. Hence the call to Roger Hansbury, a player that coach Barry Powell recalled well as a team-mate in Hong Kong and at the rather less temperate Burnley.

"Wolves came for me as a last resort - I don't think they could find anybody else!"

In fact, Hansbury made an immaculate debut in his side's 2-0 win over Hereford in front of 10,204 at Edgar Street in the Southern Area semi-final of the competition. Wolves' side was:

Hansbury; Andy Thompson; Gary Bellamy; Floyd Streete; Mark Venus; Tim Steele; Nigel Vaughan; Mick Gooding; Robbie Dennison; Steve Bull(1); Andy Mutch (1).

The area final was against Torquay.

"I enjoyed the game down there - but that one at Molineux! Oh dear! I was beaten by a free-kick when I was lining up the wall!"

The quick-thinking Mark Loram spotted Roger marshalling his troops by his left-hand post, and promptly lifted his kick into the far corner, sealing a 2-0 win for the Plainmoor side which took them to Wembley 3-2 on aggregate.

Four days later, Roger Hansbury made his League debut for Wolves in a 1-1 draw with Swansea at Molineux, Mick Stowell having been recalled to Goodison. Clean sheets followed at Huddersfield (another game for which he has zero recall!) and at home to Bristol City before Hansbury returned to St Andrews and Kendall stepped back into the fray.

"I enjoyed every minute of my spell at Molineux. It is always enjoyable to play with good players in a successful team. Training under those circumstances is a pleasure. If you're winning, then whatever you try in training seems to work. It was also good once more to be playing in front of big crowds, even though the two-sided ground meant there was less atmosphere than there should have been. Playing before big audiences never fails to remind you that there is only one place to perform - the First Division.

"I got on well with Mark Kendall - he helped me a lot. All the stick that he got - it was a shame. His confidence was all that got him through."

1989-90 started with Roger Hansbury once more confined to Birmingham's reserve side, before the opportunity came to help out struggling Colchester United. Then it was Cardiff that needed 'the flying custodian'.

"Fred Davies, himself a former Cardiff keeper, set it up. George Wood had broken his wrist and Fred recommended me to them. I spent two months down there before Dave Mackay told me they wanted me permanently. My first reaction was that I didn't want to go. I was enjoying the training at St Andrews and I felt that this was important at my stage of life. But Dave persuaded me to talk some more to Cardiff and eventually I signed. I still live in the Midlands and part of the agreement is that I go down there to train twice a week, the rest of the time it's with Birmingham.

"I have another two years on my contract at Cardiff which will take me to 38. At 33, I'd lost my appetite for the game, but it came back after a year. When you get past 30 they write you off. I told myself to dismiss all that and to enjoy what I was doing. And that's what I did at Cardiff last season. I had a good year, even though we were relegated. Nowadays I play every game as if it's my last. Sure, winning means a lot, but it's not the end if we lose.

"I want to play on after I'm 38. But I enjoy coaching and love to help Fred Davies. I've taken a course in Leisure Management. I always used to say that I'd never be a manager. But as you go on and you see how some people do it, you get to think you'd like one shot to see whether you can make a better job of things!

"I hope I still have the love of the game that Shilts has when I'm his age. His ability and determination to succeed are unbelievable. Apart from him, the keeper I most admired was, in fact, Kevin Keelan, a true entertainer. Bruce Grobbelaar reminds me of him so much."

Roger Hansbury didn't pussy-foot at all when I asked him his strengths:

"Talking, shot-stopping and bravery. I've never been strong on crosses."

Roger was amused when I suggested that this aspect of the job is perhaps the principle gauge of a goalkeeper employed by the Molineux diehards.

"You're either a natural at taking cross-balls or you're not. Peter Shilton is one of the worst in the League! But he has an understanding with his defence. They realise that he's not coming out of his six-yard box. But they also know to get out of his way on shots - they know full well he'll stop them."

Roger Hansbury unhesitatingly cites John Bond as his best manager - "such a great coach. In fact my greatest disappointment is that I did not really get to the heights that he felt I could."

Roger Hansbury, like his friend and mentor Fred Davies, is an extremely agreeable man - the sort you'd welcome as a neighbour! He and Norfolk-born wife Rosemary, who he met as a 17-year-old, live contentedly in Solihull with their children Danielle and Craig. Conversation was a joy with the still broad-Yorkshire-spoken keeper, who displayed an equal interest in his interviewer! Thus, with all genuineness, he turned the tables on me by asking 'And what are your ambitions for the future?'!

There have been better goalkeepers defending the Cow Shed end. Seldom have there been nicer ones.

PHONES

"I'll talk to you all day about Neville, but if you want to ask about my strengths then speak to someone else!"

Mike Stowell, commandingly tall, blond and personable, has emerged from the shadow of the world's best to become his own man as the most expensive goalkeeping purchase ever made by Wolverhampton Wanderers. His selection for the England 'B' squad in 1990-91 confirmed Graham Turner's foresight. His modesty, nevertheless, prevails.

"Although the record books often say otherwise, I was actually born in Portsmouth on 19th April, 1965. We were only there for a year and then it was to Bradford and Kendal before we settled at Kirkham, near Preston. Mum and dad still live there and for four years before coming to Wolverhampton I had my own house in Preston."

Mike's first school was at Freckleton, in which village his father was an officer in the open prison. Then it was to Kirkham Carr Hill School, where the young Stowell started his goalkeeping career.

"I played in goal up 'till the Under-14's and represented Lancashire Schools. But then the fourth year were struggling for forwards and another lad said he could play in goal, so I went up front. Familiar story, isn't it?! I stopped keeping altogether and played Saturdays and Sundays as a forward.

"Then I gave up the game completely for over a year. I was fed up with it really. I'd started my apprenticeship with British Telecom and the only link I had with the game was coaching a couple of kids' sides. One lad's father was connected with Freckleton from the West Lancashire League and they were struggling for keepers, so I played out that season in their reserve team. I was just 18. We won the West Lancs Reserve Division and from there I joined Kirkham, also in the West Lancs.

"After a year there, in which we won a trophy, I joined Blackpool Mechanics of the Bass North West Counties League Division Three, which was a higher standard. Once again it was for a year, towards the end of which I made some appearances for Preston's second team. Alan Kelly, the old Eire keeper, was manager and his first choice Peter Litchfield was having a bad time. One of the directors' sons, Glen Campbell, was in goals and I went into the Central League team to finish off a season in which I also played for the Telecom regional side."

Preston's new boss Tommy Booth offered the young find a one year contract but Mike declined.

"Preston were struggling and I was determined after four and a bit years to complete my telephones apprenticeship. So I joined Leyland Motors in the Bass North West Counties Division One. Of course none of their players these days work for that company, but the facilities are tremendous.

"By now Alan Kelly was running a soccer school with Alan Spavin in the States, but he came home to coach the Everton keepers. He noticed that I'd been getting good reports for Motors in the F.A. Trophy run and he came to watch us for Everton. Howard Kendall offered us a week's trial after which he asked whether I fancied turning pro. It was December 1985 and I'd been at Motors for just four months."

Stowell certainly must have impressed for he was awarded a 2½ year contract despite the fact that The Toffees already had Southall, Bobby Mimms and Neil Deamer to call upon. Mike went straight into the 'A' team in the Lancashire League Division One.

"It was a big shock! I'd been training twice a week and now it was every day. But I learned a lot. As a youngster I'd watch the senior keepers and they'd offer help now and again. As I progressed and I got to know them better, then they were even more helpful. Once I'd become second choice, Neville was fantastic. I roomed with him for a year and we became great friends."

Mike Stowell had soon established himself as an adept second choice keeper but new Goodison gaffer Colin Harvey agreed with him that it was necessary to get League experience.

"In the pre-season I'd had an operation on a finger which I'd dislocated several times previously. They took the knuckle out and fused the bones together. I was raring to go by the start of the season and Colin put us on the loan list.

"Chester came in straight away, in September 1987. Derek Fazackerley took us down to meet Harry McNally the week before and I followed behind him in my car. 'Will you be able to find it O.K. on Saturday?' he asked. I was sure I would and left in plenty of time. I was so anxious though that I completely missed the turning for the M56 and carried on down the M6. I got as far as Keele before I realised I'd gone wrong! I arrived at Sealand Road by 2.10, and Billy Stewart was dressed and changed despite his swollen ankle. Harry McNally wasn't too happy to put it mildly. But he played me and we beat Aldershot 4-1. Tony Lange was playing for them!

"We hit an unbelievable run and got to the top of the Third, the first time Chester had ever done that. We went to Roker and beat Sunderland 2-0; Gillingham had just beaten Chesterfield 10-0 and we did them 1-0."

In three months Stowell played 14 games for the Seals and returned to Goodison to find that York had moved in for him.

Bukta

"York were bottom of the Third with just one win all season. It was all rather hectic, but I enjoyed it - I enjoyed all my loan spells. We beat Chester 2-0 on New Year's Day funnily enough and I really liked working under Bobby Saxton (once upon a time a Wolves junior). My month was coming up and I was preparing to stay when Manchester City came in."

And so on February 6th 1988 Stowell made his City debut at Blackburn in a 2-1 Second Division defeat, taking over from the out-of-favour Eric Nixon. A month later came the biggest game of his career to date: an F.A. Cup Sixth Round fixture with Liverpool in front of 44,047 at Maine Road. The game was transmitted live on television and pouring rain added to the misery of the sodden young keeper as Houghton, Beardsley with a penalty, Johnston and Barnes gave the Reds a 4-0 win.

Stowell was not to blame and he retained his place until the last game of the season, a run of 14 games to add to the 6 he played for York.

"All the loan spells were educational. Every game is, of course, different. Things you do - bloody 'ell, I should've done better with that! you think afterwards. It's all very well reading textbooks but it's different on the day. There's no substitute for experience.

"Ironically I got injured playing for City reserves against Everton. I only played to help out because Eric Nixon was on his loan spell at Tranmere.

"My contract came up whilst I was at City. Every club I'd been to had shown interest in buying me but Everton kept turning them down. There was talk of a tribunal.

"But I went on tour and we started talking contracts. I signed for two more years. It was agreed that I would be number two to Neville, that I could continue to go out on loan and that if I didn't get a game for Everton we'd part company as friends."

The Toffees, however, seemed determined to recruit goalkeepers. Alec Chamberlain came from Colchester and, before him, Fred Barber from Darlington.

"When they bought Fred I was at my lowest ebb. I thought 'I'm not really wanted here'. But we've gone out on loan at the same time and I've fought my way ahead."

October 1988 saw Mike installed temporarily at Port Vale, during which stint he played in a Sherpa Van trophy game against Hereford. A little over a month later he was recalled by Everton.

"Neville had a bad back, so on the Tuesday I got my first team debut against Millwall."

In fact it was in the Simod Cup before a paltry 3,703 spectators at Goodison Park. Mike did well, however, keeping a clean sheet in a 2-0 win.

"But Nev's recovered by the Saturday! Now I'm back at Everton, though, so it's the Central League again."

Three months later enter Wolves and manager Graham Turner. Mark Kendall cannot cover his serious injury any longer and, despite heroic bravery, he steps aside as Stowell is imported for his fifth loan spell.

His debut was on March 18th 1989 as Bury are disposed of 4-0 in front of 14,828 enraptured supporters at Molineux. Wolves put out:

Stowell; Andy Thompson (Phil Robinson); Floyd Streete; Gary Bellamy; Mark Venus; Tim Steele; Mick Gooding; Nigel Vaughan; Steve Bull (3); Andy Mutch (1); Robbie Dennison (Keith Downing).

Four days later Wanderers had a Sherpa Van Southern Semi-final tie at, of all places, Hereford. It will always remain one of the great imponderables whether manager Graham Turner actually realised that his new keeper would be cup-tied for that game! Whatever the truth of the matter, Wolves decided that young Vince Bartram was not the man for the moment and snapped up a second loan keeper in Roger Hansbury. With Hereford duly defeated, back came Stowell for the next League game - at Chester! With Hansbury stepping in for the Sherpa Van, Mike Stowell was first choice for the Third Division games, including the remarkable happenings at Field Mill - on April Fools' Day!

"I like to go out early doors and have a fly around my goals for twenty minutes before the off. That day at Mansfield I suddenly felt a sharp pain in my foot. I thought I'd twisted it but when I looked there was a huge rusty nail sticking right through the boot and into my foot. The foot swelled to twice its normal size and by the end of the game I had no laces in my boot! We lost 3-1."

After a 2-1 win at Aldershot it was recall time again.

"Nev had hurt his eye this time. I was all geared up and ready to play at Tottenham when Nev turned up, his eye a lot better! I knew then that I'd have to get away. But I still had another year to run.

"1989-1990 I played all the season in Everton's Central League side, bar a couple of Third Division games for Preston. I was desperate to get away. I was frustrated being second. Of course I was always able to say that I was kept out by the best in the world, and there's no shadow of a doubt that Neville Southall is that. As I say, we got on really well - he's a great character. But sometime you have to break off, to do your own thing, to form your own identity."

For one thing, I pointed out that Mike is nowhere near as scruffy as his 'teacher'. He laughed.

"No, I suppose not - but if he's happy with that AND puts the performances in then nobody should grumble. So what, if kids copy him? It's harmless.

"Come the summer, then, my contract was up. Nev still had six years. Nev kept saying that they'd be keeping me and I'd be in - he would be off. But it's obvious - if Everton don't want to let him go then they won't. I've no regrets. If Harvey had said I'd be first choice then, yes, I'd have stayed. But he didn't, they were obviously going to keep Nev to his contract and it was time for me to go."

Thus Mike Stowell made his first permanent transfer - of course, to Wolves. Everton were quoted as wanting £750,000 whereas Wolves had thoughts of a quarter of that sum. In the end a tribunal established that the fee should be £275,000, substantially higher than the amount paid years earlier when Paul Bradshaw's signature was secured.

"I was made up, signing for Wolves. I loved my loan spell here - there's such superb team spirit. I'm looking forward to settling down for good. It'll make a nice change from all the travelling around!"

Mike moved into a home in the country, with plenty of room to walk his "good country dogs" - a springer spaniel and a golden retriever.

"That's what I enjoy."

As well, of course, as his goalkeeping.

"Eric Steele works the keepers hard and well. You need that. Firing balls at a keeper 100 times is no real benefit. You have to specialise - angles and the like. At Everton we had Jim Barron - brilliant! He ran a great school - eight of us, from Goodison, Tranmere, Wrexham and Bury."

And which goalkeeper has Mike most admired?

"Pat Jennings. He's the best I've seen - a natural. He never made anything look spectacular. But when he was around I never looked at anybody else.

"Alan Kelly was the biggest influence on my career, though. He changed things for me, obviously."

For the foresight of the great Irish international and the determination of the one time telephone engineer to become "his own man", Wolves fans will, hopefully, long be grateful.

THE QUIET ONE

After a journey though the stickiest of July evenings, the can of ice-cold Harp thrust into my hand was welcome indeed. Tony Lange, he of the piercing blue eyes, greeted me into his new Willenhall home in the Summer of 1990 with some good old East End hospitality. I was soon put at my ease.

Tony Lange was born in West Ham on 10th December 1964 and from the age of 8 or 9 was a goalkeeper, first at Poverest Junior School. From a youngster he was a fan of the local team.

"I watched all the Hammers' home games, though didn't particularly make a study of the keepers, who at the time were Bobby Ferguson and then Mervyn Day. When I was older I was playing myself so didn't get down to Upton Park too much."

Next stop was Kemnal Manor where he played for the school team. Tony Agana and Colin Foster were a year older.

"West Ham watched me as a youngster but obviously didn't reckon I was any good! But my family had moved to Orpington, where Charlton was the local club. I'd played for the school and North West Kent and was spotted as a 12-year-old by Jim Fibbins, who's still at Charlton.

"I trained with them on Tuesday evenings and then Thursdays as well when I got a bit older. I used to hate it. I'd go straight from school and by the time I got home I was absolutely knackered! Charlton didn't really cater for goalkeepers: it was all 5-a-side stuff."

Nevertheless Tony showed enough promise to sign apprentice forms at sixteen when he left school.

"I'd taken five 'O' levels, but never got 'em!"

The young Lange featured in the South East Counties League side, understudying the senior keepers Jeff Wood, Nicky Johns and, later, John Phillips.

"Mike Bailey signed me - but he was only there for two weeks afterwards! Previously he'd really got involved with the junior aspect and gave me a lift to training sometimes. A nice fella, Mike."

Lange progressed as a 17-year-old to the Football Combination when Ken Craggs was at the helm and Lenny Lawrence was reserve team manager. Before long he had become a fixture in the second team and made his senior bow on his 19th birthday at Fulham in a 1-0 Second Division win.

"I stayed in for half-a-dozen games. Nicky Johns always seemed to get injured at Christmas! They left me out for the Third Round Cup match against Colchester, but gave me a contract to soften the blow!"

Nevertheless it was back to the Reserves once Johns was fit. The following September Aldershot enquired about the possibility of taking the youngster on loan.

"I didn't know where Aldershot was! But I really enjoyed it - I'd been sick of second team football. I played seven times in the month for Aldershot but then it was back to The Valley and the reserves. That p***ed me off."

At Christmas 1984 Lenny Lawrence, now at the Valiants' helm, called Tony in again to say that Wrexham were interested.

"I spoke to them on the 'phone, but they only wanted me to sign for six months. That was no good to me -I had half a year on my contract at Charlton anyway.

"Lenny told me I'd have to pull up my socks if I wanted to stay on after those six months. As I can't do anything else except play football I thought I'd better do just that!"

In fact Lange got into the team for the Boxing Day encounter at Crystal Palace, at the time sole occupants of Selhurst Park. It was a nightmare for the young custodian, a broken ankle keeping him out for the rest of the season and demanding four operations.

"I was a bit gutted 'cos we'd drawn Spurs in the Cup AND I'd got through on merit."

Tony Lange broke through again at the end of the season in which they were promoted to the top stratum (1985-86).

"Nicky was injured once more. He and I were close, always mucking about in one another's houses. 'I think you'll be in' he told me."

He was - for a 1-0 win at top club Norwich. Lange was still there for the visit to Carlisle.

"We were 0-2 down at half time, but won 3-2 in the end, giving us promotion. That was some coach trip home, I can tell you!"

Lange didn't stay to taste First Division glory.

"Lenny offered me a new contract, except it was month-to-month on the same money because he reckoned I needed to get away. Aldershot offered me more and said I could stay in Orpington and travel down. So I signed for a year. It went well and we got promoted."

That, of course, was in the play-offs at the expense of Wolves.

"Wolves just didn't play well at all in that second leg at Molineux. I remember us arriving over so well

MANDERS
PAINT & INK

-Aldershot didn't get many big games! The coach was being led along with a police escort. The tape was playing, everyone was dancing and jigging: we were really relaxed. It was such a hot day, do you remember? I was physically sick in the dressing room beforehand (something I used to get quite a bit in my early days). I hadn't that many saves to make really. There were a couple of good catches - and I remember Bully smacking me about a bit when I made them!

"Shots had a really good side in the Fourth" (Tony talks in the classical 'Cockney', hence "Forfe", but it's too difficult to recreate through this chapter!) "Andy King was a blinding player to be with at home. Mind you, away he was a bit of a softy. There was also David Barnes and Tommy Langley, of course."

The Hampshire club struggled in the Third and were relegated after two seasons.

"I'd finished my contract and they'd offered me another two years. I felt that, at 25, it was a backward step to return to the Fourth. I thought I should try something else. So I sent off my pink form and waited for the 'phone calls. I got a few, Bristol City called every day, but Aldershot wanted £250,000, which I thought was a lot for someone who hadn't really done anything. They said it would have to go to a tribunal, but Joe Jordan didn't want any of that. I agreed terms with Plymouth, but they said they'd pull out of a tribunal if the price was too high. The tribunal was set for the Thursday, but then I got the call from Wolves.

"Bournemouth, Chelsea, Maidstone - they'd all enquired. Both Plymouth and Bristol City had offered £60,000. But I thought Aldershot were being greedy. After all, I'd gone there on a free and had given them 150 games in three years. They'd had their money's worth.

"So I came to Wolverhampton to talk to them. A big club, going places: the deal was settled in a day."

Wolves reputedly paid £150,000.

That sum, equalling the cost of Paul Bradshaw a dozen years earlier, looked trifling when Lange made a scintillating debut in the prestige friendly with Moscow Dynamo in August, 1989. The dark-haired six-footer pulled off a string of accomplished saves, immediately endearing himself to a Molineux crowd which included the legendary Bert Williams. In front of 13,998, Wolves won 3-2 with the side:

Lange; Phil Chard; Gary Bellamy; Ally Robertson; Mark Venus; Tim Steele; Nigel Vaughan; Mick Gooding (Keith Downing); Robbie Dennison (1); Steve Bull (2); Andy Mutch.

"It went quite well - I was pleased. But things got worse!"

Tony leaned forward, straightening almost compulsively the cloth adorning the dining room table which separated us. The perpetual wry smile and nervy laugh disappeared momentarily.

"I felt myself very unfortunate to be dropped. In fact I was well p***ed off! The system was changed to five at the back at the same time as I was left out, so I felt a bit peeved that I didn't get the chance to play with that system. Sure, I was disappointed with my performance in that Brighton match, especially after saving Statham's penalty against Stoke and having a fair game."

'Fair Game' was very much an understatement, Tony's heroics against the Potters being spectacular. Yet when he contrived to let the most inocuous of crosses in at his near post to set the Seagulls on the way to their 4-2 crushing of Wanderers at Molineux, manager Graham Turner decided it was time to re-instate Mark Kendall. Tony Lange never got a look in again throughout the entire season.

"Mr Turner gave his reasons for dropping me and I gave my view. Yes, we disagreed, but we didn't fall out. Mark and I got on well. The verbal he got from the crowd was unjustified - mind you, my missus Lorraine had to listen to some of the same about me in that Brighton game!

"Sure, that sort of stuff can be off-putting. Personally, though, I don't give two monkeys. I'm pleased to be doing what I do. I always like to have a smile on my face, to have a laugh and a joke.

"But getting dropped was a real low. I got so MAD, Lorraine was going to leave me! I got fed up playing in the reserves. It was almost a relief when I broke my arm near the end of the season. I kept on training and that, and the manager said he was pleased with my attitude. But the second team is no good to me, especially alternating with another keeper.

"The gaffer says he wants two experienced keepers and I can understand that, but I don't want to be a reserve forever. Believe me, it's hard turning up on a Wednesday night to play in front of a p***ing fifty people. And it's just as tough turning up on a Saturday to sit in the stand with 20,000 people and know you're not playing.

"John Phillips once told me he'd only played some 150 games in his long career, but that the money had been good. Money isn't everything.

"Yes, I DID think I should have been in the team when Mark was having all the criticism. But I never went to see the boss - if he believed I should have been in, he'd have put me in.

"I went on the list. Clubs came in for me for loan spells, but my wife had just come up to the Midlands to live and I didn't want to leave her alone, what with a baby due.

"I know I'm good enough - that's what counts. Graham Turner told me that I don't talk enough. That's true, I suppose. In fact I don't hardly talk at all. And that is one of Mark Kendall's strengths: he'd say 'I talk bollocks, but at least they hear me!'. Nicky Johns is another that never says a word. Shilton is the other extreme. Me! I'm very quiet, though the missus wouldn't agree!

"I also lark about too much. I'm not the best of trainers. But you can play anywhere with a smile on your face. I enjoy the specialist goalkeeping coaching and get on well with Eric Steele. But having a ball blasted at you from six yards in 5-a-sides is not my idea of fun.

"Strengths? A good pair of hands and a fair shot-stopper. But if you don't have those you wouldn't be a keeper, would you?

"Consistency, that's the most important part of goalkeeping. That's what the First Division keepers have. Shilton, look at him. He's done it continuously for twenty years. But Pat Jennings is the guy I admired most of all. He was so unorthodox. I guess I'm a natural like him. I don't much like hard work - in fact I don't work hardly at all! I trained very little at Aldershot, concentrating my efforts on playing. Len Walker knew that - he just let me get on with it.

"I suppose I could have stayed ten years at Aldershot and got a nice little testimonial in front of 2,000 supporters. But what do you tell the kids? I played 700 Fourth Division games? 'Why, Dad? weren't you good enough to do anything better?' My ambition is to play for as long as I can, at the highest level I can -but, above all, to be happy. Football isn't the be all and end all. Should it be? I guess I'd be lost without it and wouldn't know what to do. But family and things are more important."

As the quick-spoken Lange expounded on his philosophy of life, I couldn't help but be struck by the fact that, of all the keepers I'd met, he could most closely be likened in attitude to the man who cost Wolves exactly the same sum of money: Paul Bradshaw. Like Mark Kendall, however, Tony is ever the joker. I wasn't kidded. For all the archetypal East End chirpiness and self-avowed loathing for hard graft, the moustachioed and heavily-stubbled keeper cares deeply about his game. There is no doubt that he studies goalkeepers and goalkeeping intently and intends once more to expose his undoubted talents on a major stage. My parting wish to him was that, for the greater good of Wolverhampton Wanderers, he would challenge vigorously to maintain the highest possible custodial standards which have long been expected in the Molineux goal.

1990-91 saw Lange's frustrations continue. A brief spell back at Aldershot and a lacklustre solitary appearance as first deputy for the stricken Stowell were his closest brushes with the big time. Lange's challenge to Stowell had failed. In the summer of '92 Tony was presented with a fresh opportunity by Ossie Ardiles, with West Bromwich Albion.